Jane Eyre

CHARLOTTE BRONTË

Level 5

Retold by Evelyn Attwood
Series Editors: Andy Hopkins and Jocelyn Potter

Pearson Education Limited
Edinburgh Gate, Harlow,
Essex CM20 2JE, England
and Associated Companies throughout the world.

ISBN: 978-1-4058-6516-6

First published in the Longman Simplified English Series 1949
This adaptation first published by Addison Wesley Longman Limited
in the Longman Fiction Series 1996
First published by Penguin Books 1999
This edition published 2008

12

Text copyright © Penguin Books Ltd 1999
This edition copyright © Pearson Education Ltd 2008

Typeset by Graphicraft Ltd, Hong Kong
Set in 11/14pt Bembo
Printed in China
SWTC/12

Published by Pearson Education Ltd

Every effort has been made to trace the copyright holders and we apologise in advance
for any unintentional omissions. We would be pleased to insert the appropriate
acknowledgement in any subsequent edition of this publication.

For a complete list of the titles available in the Pearson English Readers series, please visit
www.pearsonenglishreaders.com. Alternatively, write to your local Pearson Education
office or to Pearson English Readers Marketing Department, Pearson Education,
Edinburgh Gate, Harlow, Essex CM20 2JE, England

Contents

Introduction

What crime was this, what mystery, that broke out first in fire and then in blood, in the middle of the night?

After Jane Eyre gains a position as governess to Adèle Varens at Thornfield Hall, the house of Mr Rochester, she sees the possibility of happiness for the first time in her life. But the house is full of unexplained mysteries and dangers – strange laughter comes from the top floor, and people are mysteriously attacked at night. Mr Rochester himself appears to be living with a terrible secret. Must Jane accept that she will never have a real home, and that love and understanding will never be hers?

Jane Eyre is the story of an orphan's struggle to find a place in the world. Jane's parents died when she was a baby and she knows little about her family. She is brought up by her cruel, widowed aunt, who has three children of her own. The Reeds are not pleased to have to give Jane a home, and she is treated by them with less consideration than the servants. Her life is made a misery by her cousin John and by her aunt's punishments, and she finally becomes very ill. After she expresses her great unhappiness to the doctor, she is sent away to a school for orphans. Life is very hard at Lowood Institution, too, but Jane does at least experience friendship and kindness there for the first time.

When Jane advertises for a teaching position and takes the job at Thornfield Hall, it seems that she has at last found her place in the world. But her suffering is not at an end, and she eventually finds herself again without money, possessions or a home. She wants to be valued, to find self-respect and economic independence, but the world does not expect a small, plain young woman with no family support to have ambition. Does nobody care?

Charlotte Brontë was born in Yorkshire, England in 1816, the third child in a family of writers. Their father, Patrick, was an Irishman who became the minister of a church in Haworth in 1820. Their mother, Maria Branwell, died in 1821, and her older sister came to look after the family. Mr Brontë himself educated Branwell, the only boy of the six children, at home. But their aunt was not able to deal with the girls' education and in 1824 the two oldest girls, Maria and Elizabeth, were sent away to a school for clergymen's daughters, where Charlotte and Emily joined them later. Conditions at the school were difficult and Maria and Elizabeth were taken ill and sent home, where they both died in 1825. Charlotte and Emily were then taken away from the school.

For the next five years, the four remaining children stayed at home. Branwell received lessons from his father and the girls – Charlotte, Emily and Anne – educated themselves as well as they could. The children all read widely. They saw little of other families and, to make their dull life in a small village more interesting, they began to make up stories. Many of those stories still exist today.

In 1831 Charlotte went away to school again, returning a year later to teach her sisters. She went back to the school as a teacher in 1835 and took Emily with her, but she found teaching difficult at the school and in the two positions as governess that followed. During this period she had two offers of marriage, which she refused. She was keen to open a school of her own, and in 1842 she went to Belgium with Emily to improve her French. When their aunt died, the girls returned home. Charlotte then went back to Brussels by herself but was lonely, became ill and returned to Haworth again. Her brother Branwell had failed at every job he tried and increasingly turned to alcohol and drugs. To add to her unhappiness, Charlotte's attempts to open a school in Haworth failed.

In 1846, Charlotte persuaded her sisters Emily and Anne to allow their poems to appear in a book with her own poems. The book, which they paid for themselves, was not a financial success, but they all continued to write. Charlotte's novel *Jane Eyre* came out first, in 1847, and was an immediate popular success. Later the same year, Anne's *Agnes Grey* and Emily's *Wuthering Heights* appeared.

Branwell died in September 1848. At his funeral Emily caught a fever and became very ill. She died in December. Anne died in May of the following year, at Scarborough, where she had hoped the sea air would help to improve her health. In spite of these terrible events, Charlotte continued with her writing and managed to complete two more books. She married a clergyman, A. B. Nicholls, in 1854, but died a year later. Her husband continued to look after Mr Brontë, who lived longer than all his children and died at the age of eighty-four.

The first novel that Charlotte Brontë wrote, *The Professor*, did not actually appear until 1857, after her death. It tells the story of an English teacher in a school in Brussels, and is based on Charlotte's own experiences there. *Shirley* (1849) is set in Yorkshire at a time of great industrial changes. It is a romantic story, but also comments on the lives of women at that time and tells of unrest among the cloth-makers in the area. *Villette* (1853) is set in Brussels again, in a school for young ladies, where an orphan and outsider – like Jane Eyre – becomes a teacher.

Charlotte began writing *Jane Eyre*, her most famous and popular work, in a nursing home in Manchester, where her father was receiving treatment. It is written in the first person, and is the story of a young woman's struggle to make a life for herself while keeping her self-respect and obeying her own moral principles, particularly when she falls in love with a man from a much higher class than herself. Some readers of the time were shocked that a girl as poor and plain as Jane should have the right to passionate emotions, but Jane Eyre is a woman who knows her own mind and is not afraid to express it. These readers were particularly shocked that the book was written by a woman (although the book originally came out as the work of 'Currer Bell', a name that was neither recognisably male nor female, and Charlotte's sisters also used different names to protect themselves from criticism). Most people, though, including Queen Victoria, praised the story, and it has remained popular since that time.

Society in nineteenth century England was in many ways very different from today. People were either working class, middle class or upper class and it was not possible to move from one class to another. Men worked and earned the money for their families. Women still had to obey their fathers, husbands or brothers. Working-class women could earn money as servants, but these jobs paid poorly so it was very difficult for women to be independent. Middle-class women could become governesses or teachers, which paid more. There was no National Health Service, so if someone could not pay for a doctor, their chances of recovery were very limited.

England in the nineteenth century offered few opportunities to orphans. Lacking family and money, they could not rise from poverty without the kindness of strangers. They were often treated with suspicion and punished severely. Schools for orphans usually spent little on the children's education, clothes, food and comforts. But there were people who recognized this injustice and fought for better conditions. Changes were made, as they were, eventually, to Lowood Institution in this story.

Jane Eyre was first made into a silent film in 1910, and again in 1914 and 1921. The first film with sound was in 1934. In 1944, Orson Welles played Mr Rochester and Joan Fontaine took the part of Jane. In 1996 Franco Zeffirelli directed William Hurt and

Charlotte Gainsbourg in his film of this title. Every few years a film of *Jane Eyre* is made for television, most recently in 2006.

Readers and viewers care about the poor, young governess. Will Jane find her dream of happiness, or will her only hope be cruelly destroyed?

Chapter 1   Gateshead

There was no possibility of taking a walk that day. We had, in fact, been wandering in the leafless garden for an hour in the morning, but since dinner the cold winter wind had brought with it such dark clouds and such heavy rain that further outdoor exercise was impossible.

I was glad of it; I never liked long walks, especially on cold afternoons. I hated coming home with frozen fingers and toes, with a heart saddened by the rough words of Bessie, the nurse, and by the consciousness of how weak I was, compared with Eliza, John and Georgiana Reed.

Eliza, John and Georgiana were now with their mama in the sitting room at Gateshead. She lay resting by the fireside, and with her loved ones near her (for the moment neither quarrelling nor crying) she looked perfectly happy. She had dismissed me from the group, saying that she was sorry she was forced to keep me at a distance, but that until I tried seriously to develop a more friendly and attractive nature, she really could not allow me to join in the pleasures intended only for happy little children.

'But what have I done?' I asked.

'Jane, I don't like questions or objections. Children should not speak to those older than themselves in such a way. Sit down somewhere, and until you can speak pleasantly, remain silent.'

A small breakfast room lay next to the sitting room. I slipped in there. It contained bookshelves, and I soon took possession of a book, making sure that it was one full of pictures. I climbed onto the window seat and, pulling my feet up, I sat cross-legged. I then closed the red curtains, so that I was hidden from view.

Every picture in the book told a story, often mysterious to my undeveloped understanding, but always deeply interesting – as

1

interesting as the stories of love and adventure that Bessie sometimes began on winter evenings, when she happened to be in a good humour.

With the book on my knee, I was happy. I feared nothing except interruption, and that came too soon. The voice of John Reed called me. Then there was a silence as he found the room empty.

'Where in the world is she?' he cried. 'Lizzy! Georgy!' he called to his sisters. 'Jane is not here. Tell Mama she has run out into the rain. Bad creature!'

'It is lucky that I closed the curtain,' I thought, and I hoped with all my heart that he would not discover my hiding place. He would not in fact have found it by himself, as he was neither sharp-sighted nor intelligent, but Eliza put her head round the door, and said:

'She is in the window seat, surely, John.'

I came out immediately, because I trembled at the idea of being dragged out by John.

'What do you want?' I asked.

'Say, "What do you want, Master Reed?" ' was the answer. 'I want you to come here.' Seating himself in an armchair, he made a sign to me to move closer and stand in front of him.

John Reed was a schoolboy of fourteen years, four years older than I was; he was large and fat for his age, with an unhealthy skin, unattractive features and thick arms and legs. He ought now to have been at school, but his mama had brought him home for a month or two, "on account of his delicate health". His schoolmaster said that his condition would improve if he received fewer cakes and sweets from his family, but his mother's heart found such a severe opinion unacceptable, and she preferred to believe that he worked too hard and missed his home.

John was not very fond of his mother and sisters, and he hated

2

me. He treated me badly, and punished me, not two or three times a week, nor once or twice a day, but continually. I had no protection from him; the servants did not like to offend their young master, and Mrs Reed never appeared to see him strike me or to hear him insult me.

Having learnt to be obedient to John, I came up to his chair. He spent about three minutes in putting out his tongue at me. I knew that he would hit me soon, and while I waited fearfully for the blow, I thought about his disgustingly ugly appearance. I wonder whether he read my mind in my face; suddenly, without speaking, he struck me sharply and hard. I almost fell, and when I was upright again, I stepped back from his chair.

'That is for questioning Mama,' he said, 'and for hiding like a thief behind curtains, and for the look you had in your eyes two minutes ago, you rat!'

I was so used to John Reed's insults that I never had any idea of replying to them. My anxiety was about how to receive the blow that would certainly follow.

'What were you doing behind the curtain?' he asked.

'I was reading.'

'Show me the book.'

I returned to the window and brought it in silence.

'You have no right to take our books. You are a poor relation, Mama says. You have no money; your father left you none. You ought to beg, and not live here with gentlemen's children like us, and eat the same meals as we do, and wear clothes that our mama has to pay for. Now, I'm warning you not to touch my bookshelves again, because they *are* mine. The whole house is mine, or will be in a few years. Go and stand by the door, out of the way of the mirror and the windows.'

I did so, not at first realizing his intention. When I saw him lift and balance the book and stand in the act of aiming it, though, I jumped to one side with a cry of fear. Not soon enough. The book was thrown, it hit me, and I fell, striking my head against the door and cutting it. The cut bled, and the pain was sharp. My fear had by now passed its limit, and other feelings took its place.

'Wicked and cruel boy!' I said. 'You are like a murderer – you are like a slave driver – you are like the evil rulers of ancient Rome!'

'What! What!' he cried. 'Did she say that to me? Did you hear her, Eliza and Georgiana? I'll tell Mama! But first–'

He ran straight at me. I felt him seize my hair and shoulder, but now I was desperate; I really thought him a murderer. I felt a drop or two of blood from my head running down my neck, and my sense of suffering for the moment was stronger than my fear. I fought him madly. I am not sure what I did with my hands, but he called me 'Rat! Rat!' and screamed loudly. Help was near; his sisters had run for Mrs Reed, who had gone upstairs. Now she came on the scene, followed by Bessie and by Abbot, one of the servant girls. We were separated. I heard the words:

'Oh! What a wicked little thing, to fly at Master John like that!'

'Did anybody ever see such evil passion!'

Then Mrs Reed commanded:

'Take her away to the red room, and lock her in there.' Four hands seized me, and I was carried upstairs.

Chapter 2   The Red Room

I fought all the way. This was unusual for me, and greatly strengthened the bad opinion of me that Bessie and Abbot already held.

'Hold her arms. She's like a mad cat.'

'For shame! For shame!' cried Abbot. 'What terrible behaviour, Miss Eyre, to strike a young gentleman, your guardian's son – your young master!'

'Master! How is he my master? Am I a servant?'

'No, you are less than a servant, because you do nothing to support yourself. There, sit down, and think over your wickedness.'

They had got me by this time into the room named by Mrs Reed, and had pushed me onto a chair. I began to rise from it again, but their two pairs of hands prevented me.

'If you don't sit still, you must be tied down,' said Bessie. 'Miss Abbot, lend me your belt. She would break mine immediately.'

'Don't do that,' I cried. 'I will not move.'

'Take care that you don't,' said Bessie, and when she had made sure that I really was becoming quieter, she loosened her hold on me. She and Abbot stood with folded arms, looking darkly and doubtfully at my face.

'She never did this before,' said Bessie at last, turning to Abbot.

'But it was always in her,' was the reply. 'I've often given Mrs Reed my opinion of the child, and she agrees with me. She's a deceitful little thing.'

Bessie did not answer, but before long she addressed me and said:

'You ought to know, miss, that you should be grateful to Mrs Reed. She supports you. If she were to send you away, who would look after you?'

I had nothing to say to these words. They were not new to me. I had heard many suggestions of the same kind before, very painful and wounding to my pride, but only half understood. Abbot joined in:

'And you ought not to think yourself equal to the two Misses Reed and Master Reed, just because Mrs Reed kindly allows you to be brought up with them. They will have a great deal of money in the future, and you will have none. It is your duty to be grateful, and to behave well.'

'What we tell you is for your own good,' added Bessie in a softer voice. 'You should try to be useful and to please them. Then, perhaps, you will have a home here. But if you become angry and rude, Mrs Reed will send you away, I am sure.'

'Besides,' said Abbot, 'God will punish you. He might strike you dead in the middle of your anger. Come, Bessie, we will leave her. Say your prayers, Miss Eyre, because if you are not sorry for your wickedness, something bad might come down the chimney and take you away.'

They went, shutting the door and locking it behind them.

The red room was a square bedroom with dark wooden furniture, a heavy red rug, a very large bed, and red curtains always closed across the windows. This room was cold, because it rarely had a fire; silent, because it was far from the nursery and the kitchen; frightening, because it was rarely entered. It was here that Mr Reed had died nine years before.

I was not quite sure whether they had locked the door, and when I dared to move, I went to see. Ah, yes! There had never been a surer prison.

My head still ached and bled from the blow that I had received and my fall. No one had blamed John for striking me without cause. 'Unjust! Unjust!' I thought. I began to plan some escape, such as running away, or never eating or drinking any more, and letting myself die.

It was past four o'clock, and daylight began to leave the red room. I heard the rain beating against the windows, and the wind crying in the trees behind the house. Gradually I became as cold as a stone, and then my courage sank. Everyone said that I was wicked, and perhaps I was.

My thoughts turned to my uncle. I could not remember him, but I knew that he was my mother's brother, that he had taken me as a parentless baby to his house, and that before he died he had received a promise from his wife, Mrs Reed, that she would look after me as one of her own children.

A strange idea entered my head. I never doubted that if Mr Reed had been alive, he would have treated me kindly, and now, in the growing darkness, I began to remember stories of dead men, troubled in their graves by the knowledge that their last wishes were not carried out, revisiting the earth. Perhaps Mr Reed's ghost might rise before me. This idea, instead of comforting me, filled me with fear. At this moment, a beam of light shone on the wall. Probably it was from a lamp carried outside across the garden, but to my shaken nerves, prepared for terror, it appeared like a sign of someone coming from another world. My heart beat fast, my head became hot. A sound filled my ears, which seemed like the rushing of wings. I ran in despair to the door and shook the lock. Footsteps came hurrying along the outer passage, the key was turned, and Bessie and Abbot entered.

'Miss Eyre, are you ill?' said Bessie.

'What a terrible noise! It went right through me!' cried Abbot.

'Take me out! Let me go into the nursery!' I begged.

'What for? Are you hurt? Have you seen something?' Bessie demanded again.

'Oh, I saw a light, and I thought a ghost had come.' I had now got hold of Bessie's hand, and she did not take it from me.

'She has screamed on purpose,' Abbot said in disgust. 'And what a scream! If she had been in great pain, there would have been some excuse for it, but she only wanted to bring us all here. I know her wicked tricks.'

'What is all this?' demanded another voice sharply. Mrs Reed was coming along the passage. 'Abbot and Bessie, I believe I gave orders that Jane Eyre should be left in the red room until I came to her myself.'

'Miss Jane screamed so loud, madam,' replied Bessie.

'Let her go,' was the only answer. 'Loose Bessie's hand, child; you cannot succeed in getting out by these means. I hate tricks, especially in children. It is my duty to show you that they will not succeed. You will stay here an hour longer, and it is only on condition of perfect obedience and silence that I shall let you out then.'

'Oh, Aunt! Have pity! Forgive me! I cannot bear it! Let me be punished in some other way!'

'Be quiet! This passion is almost disgusting.' She did not believe in my sincerity, and really thought that I was pretending.

Bessie and Abbot left us, and Mrs Reed pushed me roughly and impatiently back into my prison and locked me in without a further word. I heard her go away, and soon after she had left my head seemed to go round and round and I fell to the ground in a faint.

Chapter 3 Illness

The next thing I remember is waking up feeling as if I had had a fearful dream, and seeing in front of me a terrible bright red light, crossed with thick black bars. I heard voices, too, speaking with a hollow sound. Uncertainty and fear confused my senses. Then I became conscious that someone was lifting me up more gently than I had ever been raised before. I rested my head against an arm, and felt comfortable.

In five minutes the cloud of confusion melted away. I knew quite well that I was in my own bed, and that the red light came from the nursery fire. It was night: a candle burnt on the table. Bessie stood at the foot of the bed with a bowl in her hand, and a gentleman sat in a chair beside me, leaning over me.

I experienced a warm feeling of protection and safety when I knew that there was a stranger in the room, a person not belonging to Gateshead and not related to Mrs Reed. Turning from Bessie, I examined the face of the visitor. I knew him; it was Mr Lloyd, who sold medicines and who was sometimes called in by Mrs Reed when one of the servants was ill. For herself and her children she employed a proper doctor.

'Well, who am I?' he asked.

I spoke his name, offering him my hand at the same time. He took it, smiling and saying, 'You will be better soon.' He then addressed Bessie, warning her to be very careful that I was left in peace during the night. Having given some further directions, he left, saying that he would call again the next day.

'Do you feel as if you could sleep, miss?' asked Bessie, rather softly.

I hardly dared answer her, as I feared that her next sentence might be rough.

'I will try.'

'Would you like to drink, or could you eat anything?'

'No, thank you, Bessie.'

'Then I think I will go to bed, but you may call me if you need anything in the night.'

Bessie went into the room of another servant, which was near. I heard her say:

'Sarah, come and sleep with me in the nursery. I daren't be alone with that poor child tonight: she might die. It's strange that she should have fainted so. I wonder if she saw anything. Mrs Reed was rather too hard on her.'

Sarah came back with her, and after half an hour of whispering together, they both fell asleep. For me, though, it was a night of wakefulness.

Next day, I was up and dressed by twelve o'clock, and sat wrapped in a rug by the nursery fire. I felt physically weak, but my worst trouble was an indescribable misery of mind. But, I thought, I ought to have been happy, as all the Reeds had gone out in the carriage. Abbot was sewing in another room and Bessie, as she moved around the nursery at her work, spoke to me now and then with unusual kindness. Then, too, a cake had come up from the kitchen, on a certain brightly painted plate which I had loved for a long time but had been forbidden to touch. This beautiful dish was now placed on my knee, and I was invited to eat. Unfortunately, though, I had no desire to eat. Bessie asked whether I would like a book, and I begged her to fetch *Gulliver's Travels* from the library. I had read this book again and again with joy, but when it was now placed in my hands, the pictures that had so often given me pleasure, the very large and the very small men, filled my mind with fear. I closed the book.

Bessie had now finished tidying, and began to sew. At the same time, she sang. She had a sweet voice, but the song was a sad one, about an orphan child, and my tears began to flow.

'Come, Miss Jane, don't cry,' said Bessie, as it ended. She might just as well have said to the fire, 'Don't burn!'

Shortly after that, Mr Lloyd came in.

'What, up already!' he said, as he entered the nursery. 'Well, nurse, how is she?'

Bessie answered that I was doing very well.

'Then she ought to look more cheerful. Come here, Miss Jane. You have been crying: can you tell me why? Have you any pain?'

'No, sir.'

'Oh, I suppose she is crying because she could not go out in the carriage with Mrs Reed,' said Bessie.

I answered immediately, 'I never cried for such a thing in my life! I hate going out in the carriage. I cry because I am miserable.'

'Nonsense, miss!' said Bessie.

Mr Lloyd appeared a little puzzled. He fixed his eyes on me very steadily. Having looked at me for some time, he said:

'What made you ill yesterday?'

'She had a fall,' said Bessie, again entering the conversation.

'Fall! Why, that is like a baby! Can't she manage to walk at her age?'

'I was knocked down,' was my explanation, drawn from me by my wounded pride. 'But that did not make me ill.'

At that moment a loud bell rang for the servants' dinner. 'That's for you, nurse,' said Mr Lloyd. 'You can go down.' Bessie would rather have stayed, but she had to go because Mrs Reed was firm that everyone should attend meals on time.

'The fall did not make you ill. What did, then?' continued Mr Lloyd when Bessie had gone.

'I was shut up in a room where there is a ghost.'

I saw Mr Lloyd smile and look puzzled at the same time.

'Ghost! So, you are a baby, after all! You are afraid of ghosts?'

'Of Mr Reed's ghost. He died in that room. Neither Bessie nor anyone else will go into it at night, if they can avoid it. It was cruel to shut me up alone without a candle.'

'And is it that which makes you so miserable?'

'I am unhappy for other reasons.'

'What other reasons? Can you tell me some of them?'

How difficult it is for a child to reply to such a question, but how much I wanted to try!

'For one thing, I have no father or mother, brothers or sisters.'

'But you have a kind aunt and cousins.'

'But John Reed knocked me down, and my aunt shut me up in the red room.'

Mr Lloyd looked thoughtful.

'Don't you think Gateshead is a very beautiful place?' he asked. 'Aren't you very lucky to be able to live here?'

'It is not my house, sir, and Abbot says I have less right here than a servant.'

'But you wouldn't wish to leave such a lovely place?'

'If I had anywhere else to go, I should be glad to leave it.'

'Have you any other relations belonging to your father?'

'I don't know. I asked Aunt Reed once, and she said that possibly I might have some poor, low relations called Eyre, but she knew nothing of them.'

'Would you like to go to school?'

I considered. I hardly knew what school was. John Reed hated his school, and spoke insultingly of his master, but John Reed's opinions were not mine. Bessie's accounts of school rules, based on the experiences of the young ladies of a family where she lived before coming to Gateshead, were rather frightening, but her details of the skills gained by these young ladies were attractive. She spoke proudly of the beautiful paintings of scenery and flowers that they did, of songs that they could sing, of music they could play, of French books that they could translate, until my spirit was moved to jealousy. Besides, school would be a complete change, the beginning of a new life.

'I would very much like to go to school,' I said at last.

'Well, who knows what may happen?' said Mr Lloyd, getting up. As Bessie returned at that moment, he said to her:

'Is Mrs Reed back yet? I would like to speak to her before I go.'

That night, when Bessie and Abbot sat sewing in the nursery, supposing me to be asleep, I learnt from their conversation that Mr Lloyd had persuaded Mrs Reed to send me to school. On the same occasion I heard for the first time, from Abbot's information to Bessie, that my father had been a poor clergyman, whom my mother had married against the wishes of her friends; that my grandfather had been so angry at her disobedience that he had left her nothing when he died; that after a year of marriage my father had caught a bad fever while visiting the poor, that my mother had caught the disease from him, and that both had died soon after.

Chapter 4   Mr Brocklehurst

It was 15 January at about nine o'clock in the morning. Bessie had gone down to breakfast, and my cousins had not yet been sent for by their mama. Eliza was putting on her hat and coat to go and feed her chickens, a job of which she was fond, since she sold the eggs to the housekeeper at a good profit. Georgiana was putting artificial flowers in her hair. I was making my bed, as Bessie frequently employed me as a sort of additional servant.

The main gates could be seen from the nursery window, and at this moment they were thrown open and a carriage rolled through. It stopped in front of the house, the doorbell rang loudly, and the newcomer was admitted. Bessie came running upstairs.

'Miss Jane, what are you doing? Have you washed your face and hands this morning?'

She brushed my hair hurriedly, and told me to go down immediately, as I was wanted in the breakfast room.

I went slowly downstairs. It was a long time since I had been called to Mrs Reed's presence. Fearful and trembling, I stood outside the door of the breakfast room. What a miserable little creature fear had made me!

'Who could want me?' I wondered. 'Whom shall I see besides Aunt Reed in the room? A man or a woman?'

I turned the handle, opened the door, and passing through looked up at – a black pillar! That, at least, was how the straight, narrow shape, standing upright on the rug, appeared to me at first sight. Even the severe face at the top seemed to be cut from stone.

Mrs Reed was in her usual seat by the fire. She made a sign to me to come closer, saying to the stranger:

'This is the little girl about whom I wrote to you.'

He (it was a man) turned his head slowly and, having

13

examined me, said in a deep, serious voice:

'She is small. What is her age?'

'Ten years.'

'So much?' he said, in surprise. In a while he addressed me:

'Your name, little girl?'

'Jane Eyre, sir.'

'Well, Jane Eyre, and are you a good child?'

I was silent. Mrs Reed answered for me with a shake of her head.

'There is no sight so sad as a bad child,' he continued. 'God will punish the wicked. Do you say your prayers night and morning?'

'Yes, sir.'

Mrs Reed then entered the conversation.

'Mr Brocklehurst, I believe I informed you in the letter that I wrote to you three weeks ago that this little girl has not quite the character she ought to have. If you would admit her to Lowood, I would be glad if the teachers would keep a strict eye on her, and, above all, guard against her worst fault, a tendency to deceit.'

I had good reason to hate and fear Mrs Reed, because it was in her nature to wound my feelings cruelly. This criticism, made before a stranger, cut me to the heart. I saw that she was doing her best to spoil for me the new life from which I hoped so much.

'Deceit is certainly a sad fault in a child,' said Mr Brocklehurst. 'She shall be watched, Mrs Reed. I will speak to Miss Temple and the teachers.'

'I wish her to be brought up in a manner suited to her future,' continued my aunt, 'to be made useful. As for the holidays, she will, with your permission, spend them all at Lowood.'

'Your decisions are wise, madam. Little girl, here is a book. Read especially the part containing an account of the sudden death of Martha, a wicked child who told lies.'

Shortly after that, he left, and Mrs Reed and I were alone together. Some minutes passed in silence. She was sewing. I was watching her. A passion of anger burned in my heart.

Mrs Reed looked up. Her eyes settled on mine, and her fingers stopped working.

'Go out of the room. Return to the nursery,' was her command.

I got up, and went to the door. Then I came back again across the room, close to her.

I had to speak, but what strength had I to strike back at this enemy of mine? I called on all my energies, and began my attack:

'I am not deceitful. If I were, I would say I loved you, but I do not love you. I dislike you more than anyone in the world, except John Reed. And this book about the liar, you may give it to your girl Georgiana, because it is she who tells lies, not I.'

Mrs Reed's hand lay still on her work, and her cold eye remained fixed on mine.

'What more have you to say?' she asked, rather in the voice in which a person might address someone of the same age than that used to a child.

Shaking from head to foot, trembling with uncontrolled excitement, I went on:

'I am glad you are no relation of mine. I will never call you Aunt again as long as I live. If anyone asks me how I liked you, and how you treated me, I will say that you treated me with miserable cruelty. You have no pity.'

'How dare you say that, Jane Eyre!'

'How dare I, Mrs Reed? Because it is the truth. You think I have no feelings, and can live without one bit of love and kindness. I shall remember how you pushed me back into the red room, though I was frightened and begged you to have pity on me. And that punishment you made me suffer because your wicked boy struck me – knocked me down for nothing. People think you are a good woman, but you are bad, hard-hearted!'

Before I had finished this reply, my soul began to feel the strangest sense of freedom. It was not without cause. Mrs Reed looked frightened. Her work had slipped from her knee. She was even twisting her face as if she was going to cry.

'Jane, you are mistaken. What is the matter with you? Why are you trembling so violently? Would you like some water?'

'No, Mrs Reed.'

'Is there anything else you wish for, Jane? Believe me, I desire to be your friend.'

'Not you. You told Mr Brocklehurst that I had a bad character, and I will let everyone at Lowood know what you are, and what you have done.'

'Jane, you don't understand these things. Children must be corrected for their faults.'

'Deceit is not my fault!'

'But you must admit that you are passionate. Now return to the nursery, my dear, and lie down a little.'

'I am not your dear. Send me to school soon, Mrs Reed, because I hate to live here.'

'I will certainly send her to school soon,' murmured Mrs Reed to herself and, picking up her work, she suddenly left the room.

Chapter 5   A Journey

Five o'clock had hardly struck on the morning of 19 January, when Bessie brought a candle into my little room and found me already up and dressed. I was leaving Gateshead that day by a coach that passed the house at six o'clock. Bessie had lit a fire in the nursery, where she now began to get my breakfast. Few children can eat when excited at the thought of a journey. I could not. When Bessie had urged me unsuccessfully to take a few spoonfuls of the boiled milk and bread that she had prepared for me, she wrapped up some cake in paper and put it in my bag. Then she helped me to put on my coat and hat, and we left the nursery.

As we passed Mrs Reed's bedroom, Bessie said:

'Will you go in and say goodbye to Mrs Reed?'

'No, Bessie. She came to my bed last night when you had gone down to supper, and said I need not wake her in the morning, or my cousins either; and she told me to remember that she had always been my best friend.'

'What did you say, miss?'

'Nothing. I covered my face with the sheet, and turned from her to the wall.'

'That was wrong, Miss Jane.'

'Goodbye to Gateshead!' I cried, as we passed through the hall and went out of the front door.

It was very dark, and Bessie carried a lamp. The winter morning was wet and cold as I hurried to the gate. My box, which had been carried there the night before, stood ready. It was only a few minutes to six, and shortly after our arrival there, the distant roll of wheels announced that the coach was coming. There it was, with its four horses, and its top loaded with passengers. The coachman and the guard loudly urged me to hurry, my box was lifted up, and I was taken from Bessie's neck, on which I hung with kisses.

'Be sure and take good care of her,' she cried to the guard, as he lifted me inside.

The door was closed. In this way I was separated from Bessie and Gateshead – in this way carried away to unknown and, as it seemed to me, far-off and mysterious places.

I remember very little of the journey. I only know that the day seemed endless, and that we appeared to travel over hundreds of miles of road. We passed through several towns, and in one large one the coach stopped, the horses were taken away to find water, and the passengers got down to eat. I was carried into a small hotel where the guard wanted me to have some food, but I could not manage anything. He left me in a large room, where I walked up and down, greatly afraid of someone coming and taking me away, because I had heard about children being stolen in many of Bessie's stories.

We continued on our way. The wet, misty afternoon grew darker. We passed through no more towns. The scenery was different, and great grey hills appeared in the distance. We drove down a valley, dark with woods.

At last I fell asleep, but soon the stopping of the coach woke me. The door was open, and a person was standing beside it. I saw her face and dress by the light of the lamps.

'Is there a little girl called Jane Eyre here?' she asked.

I answered, 'Yes,' and was lifted out. My box was handed down, and the coach immediately drove away.

I was stiff from sitting so long, and confused with the noise and movement of the coach. I looked around me. Rain, wind and darkness filled the air, but I saw faintly in front of me a wall, and a door open in it. Through this door I passed with my new guide. A house with many windows, in some of which lights were burning, could now be seen. We went up a broad path and through a door; then I was led through a passage into a room with a fire, and left alone.

Chapter 6   Lowood Institution

After warming my frozen fingers over the fire, I looked around the room. It was a sitting room, not so grand as the one at Gateshead, but comfortable enough.

A tall lady entered, followed by another.

'The child is very young to be sent alone,' said the first. She looked at me for a minute, and then added, 'She had better be put to bed soon. She looks tired. Are you tired?' She placed her hand on my shoulder as she spoke.

'A little.'

'And hungry too, no doubt. Let her have some supper before she goes to bed, Miss Miller. Is this the first time you have left your parents to come to school, little girl?'

I explained that I had no parents. She asked me how long they had been dead, then my age, my name, and whether I could read, write and sew a little. Then she touched my face gently with her finger, and saying that she hoped I would be a good child, she dismissed me together with Miss Miller.

The lady whom we now left was, as I afterwards learnt, Miss Temple, the head teacher, who was in charge of the school. Miss Miller looked younger and more ordinary. She seemed tired. Led by her, I passed through rooms and along passages until I heard the murmur of many voices and entered a wide, long room with great tables, two at each end, on each of which burnt a pair of candles. Seated all round was a collection of girls of every age, from nine or ten to twenty. They were all dressed in brown. It was the hour of study, and they were preparing their work for the next day.

Miss Miller made a sign to me to sit down. Then, walking to the top of the room, she cried out:

'Collect the lesson books and put them away.'

Four tall girls rose from different tables and, going round, picked up the books and removed them. Miss Miller again gave the word of command:

'Fetch the supper.'

The tall girls went out and returned in a short time, each carrying a plate, with pieces of bread arranged on it, and a container of water. The bread was handed round, and those who wanted took a drink of water. When it came to my turn I drank, as I was thirsty, but I was too tired to eat.

When the meal was over, prayers were said, and the classes moved off in order, two by two, upstairs. I could hardly keep awake, and I did not notice what sort of a place the bedroom was, except that like the schoolroom it was very long. Miss Miller helped me to undress. Each of the long rows of beds was quickly filled, and in ten minutes the single light was put out.

The night passed rapidly. I was too tired even to dream. When I opened my eyes, a loud bell was ringing. The girls were up and dressing. Daylight had not yet appeared, and a light burned in the room. I, too, rose and dressed. It was bitterly cold. I washed when I found a bowl not in use, which was not for some time since there was only one for every six girls. Again the bell rang. All formed in line, two by two, and in that order went downstairs and entered the cold and badly lit schoolroom. Here prayers were said and Miss Miller afterwards called out: 'Form classes.'

A great amount of noise and movement followed for several minutes, during which Miss Miller repeatedly cried, 'Silence!' and 'Order!' When it had ended, I saw that the girls were arranged in four half-circles, each around a table and chair. All held books in their hands, and a large book lay on each table. A pause followed. Miss Miller walked from one class to another, silencing the whisperers.

A distant bell sounded. Immediately three ladies entered the room. Each walked to a table, and Miss Miller took the fourth one, round which the smallest children were waiting. I was now called to this lowest class.

Work began with a long reading of the Bible. By the time that was over, daylight had come. The bell sounded once more, and the classes marched into another room for breakfast. How glad I was at the thought of getting something to eat! I was now nearly sick from emptiness, having eaten so little the day before.

The dining-room tables were set with steaming bowls of something hot, but to my disappointment the smell was not inviting. I saw universal signs of misery, and from the front the tall girls in the first class began to murmur:

'Disgusting! The soup is burnt again!'

A prayer was said, then a servant brought in some tea for the teachers, and the meal began.

Violently hungry, and now very faint, I eagerly ate a spoonful of my soup without thinking of the taste, but when I had satisfied the first sharpness of hunger, I could eat no more. All around me, the spoons moved slowly. I saw each girl taste her soup and try to swallow it, but in most cases the attempt was soon ended.

When another prayer had been said, we returned to the schoolroom. I was one of the last to go out, and as I passed the tables, I saw one teacher take a bowl of the soup and taste it. She looked at the others. All their faces expressed displeasure.

A quarter of an hour passed before lessons began again, during which everyone talked loudly and freely. Every conversation was about the breakfast. I heard the name of Mr Brocklehurst mentioned by some. Miss Miller shook her head disapprovingly, but she did not attempt to stop the general complaints. No doubt she sympathized with us.

At nine o'clock there was a sudden silence. The head teacher had entered. She called the first class around her, and gave a lesson on countries of the world. The lower classes worked with the other teachers at history and grammar, then writing and sums followed, and music lessons were given to some of the older girls by Miss Temple.

At last the clock struck twelve. Miss Temple rose.

'I have a word to address to the pupils,' she said. 'This morning you had a breakfast which you could not eat. I have ordered that a meal of bread and cheese shall be served to you all.'

The teachers looked at her in surprise.

'It is to be done on my responsibility,' she added, and then left the room.

The bread and cheese were soon brought in and handed round, to the joy of the whole school. The order was then given, 'To the garden!' Following the crowd, I found my way out of doors.

The garden was a wide enclosure with high walls around it. A middle space was divided into a number of little squares, which were given to each pupil as gardens to look after. When they were full of flowers, they would no doubt look pretty, but now it was winter. The stronger girls ran about and played games, but many pale and thin ones crowded together for shelter and warmth in a covered place at the end, and I often heard these coughing in the misty air.

I had not yet spoken to anyone, and no one took any notice of me. I stood there feeling lonely enough, but I was used to being apart from others. I leaned against a pillar of the shelter and watched, trying to forget the cold. I looked up at the house. Over the door the following words were cut in stone:

LOWOOD INSTITUTION
THIS SCHOOL WAS BUILT BY
NAOMI BROCKLEHURST
OF BROCKLEHURST HALL

I read these words several times, and as I did so, a cough sounded behind me. I turned my head and saw a girl sitting on a stone seat reading. While turning over a page, she happened to look up, and I said to her directly:

'Is your book interesting?'

'I like it,' she answered, after a pause of a moment or two in which she examined me.

'What is it about?'

'You may look at it,' the girl replied, offering me the book. I, too, liked reading, but I soon saw that this was too difficult for me. I returned it to her, and she received it quietly. She was about to go on with her story, but again I interrupted her.

'Can you tell me what the writing on that stone over the door means? What is Lowood Institution?'

'This house that you have come to live in. I suppose you are an orphan, aren't you?'

'Both my parents died before I can remember.'

'Well, all the girls in this school have lost either one or both parents. This is a place for educating orphans.'

'Do we pay no money? Do they keep us for nothing?'

'We pay, or our friends pay, fifteen pounds a year. It is not enough, and the rest is supplied by generous ladies and gentlemen in this neighbourhood and in London.'

'Who is Naomi Brocklehurst?'

'The lady who built most of this house, and whose son controls and directs everything here.'

'Then this house does not belong to the tall lady who said we could have bread and cheese?'

'To Miss Temple? Oh, no! I wish it did. She is responsible to Mr Brocklehurst for everything that she does here. Mr Brocklehurst buys all our food and clothes.'

'Is he a good man?'

'He is a clergyman.'

'Do you like the teachers?'

'Well enough.'

I asked about their names and characters, how long she had been at the school and, last of all, whether she was happy there.

'You ask rather too many questions. Now I want to read.'

But at that moment the bell rang, and we all reentered the house. Dinner was served in two large metal dishes, from which came a strong smell of bad fat, not much better than that at breakfast time. The mixture was made up of greyish potatoes and strange bits of fatty brown meat cooked together. I ate what I could, and wondered whether meals would be like this every day.

After dinner, there were more lessons until five o'clock.

The only event of the afternoon was that I saw the girl with whom I had talked dismissed from a history class and sent to stand in the middle of the large classroom. The punishment seemed to me deeply wounding to one's pride, and especially for such a big girl – she looked thirteen years or more. To my surprise, she neither cried nor turned red with embarrassment.

'How can she bear it so quietly?' I asked myself. 'She looks as if she were thinking of something beyond her punishment. She is in a world of private dreams, not here with us. I wonder what sort of a girl she is – good or bad.'

Soon after five o'clock, we had another meal. This was a cup of coffee and half a piece of brown bread. I ate eagerly, but I remained hungry. Half an hour's play followed, then study, then the cup of water and piece of bread, prayers and bed. That was my first day at Lowood.

Chapter 7   Helen Burns

The next day began as before, with getting up and dressing before sunrise, but this morning it was so cold that we were unable to wash, since the water was frozen in the bowls.

Before the long hour of Bible-reading was over, I thought I would die of cold. Breakfast time came at last, and this morning the soup was not burnt. The quality was satisfactory, but the quantity small. How I wished that my share were doubled!

In the course of the day, I began to work as a member of the fourth class. At first, because I had not been used to learning by heart, the lessons seemed to me both long and difficult. The frequent change from one subject to another also confused me, and I was glad when at about three o'clock in the afternoon Miss Smith put some sewing into my hands and sent me to a quiet corner of the schoolroom. At that hour most of the others were also sewing, but one class still stood round a teacher reading, and as the room was quiet, the subject of their lesson could be heard, together with the answers of the pupils and the remarks of the teacher. It was history, and I noticed my companion of the day before at the top of the class, until for some mistake she was sent right to the bottom. Even then, she was continually spoken to in such words as these:

'Burns,' (this was her name: the girls here were all called by their family names) 'you are standing on the side of your shoe. Turn your toes out immediately.' 'Burns, hold your head up.' 'Burns, pull your chin in.'

When a chapter had been read through twice, the books were closed and the girls examined. Most of them seemed to find it difficult, but Burns was ready with answers on every point. I kept expecting the teacher, Miss Scatcherd, to praise her, but instead she suddenly cried out:

'You dirty, unpleasant girl! You have not cleaned your nails this morning!'

Burns made no answer. I was surprised at her silence.

'Why,' I thought, 'does she not explain that the water was frozen this morning?'

My attention was now called for by Miss Smith, who wanted to look at my work. When I returned to my seat, Burns was just leaving the room in obedience to some order from Miss Scatcherd. She returned half a minute later carrying in her hand a number of sticks tied together at one end. These she gave respectfully to the teacher. Miss Scatcherd immediately hit her with them sharply across her neck. Not one tear rose in Burns's eye and, while I paused in my sewing because my fingers trembled with anger at this scene, not one feature of her thoughtful face changed its expression.

During the play hour that evening, I made my way to the

fireplace. There, kneeling by it, I found Burns, her attention fixed on a book.

'Is that the same one as yesterday?' I asked.

'Yes, I have just finished it.' She shut it.

'What is your name besides Burns?'

'Helen.'

'Do you come from far away, Helen?'

'I come from a place further north, on the borders of Scotland.'

'You must wish to leave Lowood.'

'No, why should I? I was sent here to get an education, and it would be no use going away before I had done so.'

'But that teacher, Miss Scatcherd, is so cruel to you.'

'Cruel? Not at all! She is severe. She dislikes my faults.'

'If I were in your place, and she struck me, I would get the sticks from her hand, and break them under her nose.'

'If you did, Mr Brocklehurst would send you away from the school, and that would make your relations very unhappy.'

'But it seems to me shameful to be beaten in front of everyone. I could not bear it.'

'It is weak and silly to say that you cannot bear what it is necessary for you to bear.'

I heard her with wonder and tried to understand.

'You say you have faults, Helen. What are they? To me you seem very good.'

'I am, as Miss Scatcherd says, careless and untidy. I rarely keep things in order. I forget rules. I read when I ought to be learning my lessons.'

'Is Miss Temple as severe with you as Miss Scatcherd?'

A soft smile came over her face.

'Miss Temple is full of goodness. She sees my faults, and tells me them gently. When I do anything well, she praises me generously.'

'And when Miss Temple teaches you, do your thoughts wander?'

'No, not often, because what she says is generally so interesting to me.'

'You are good to those who are good to you. That is all I ever desire to be. But when we are struck without a reason, we should strike back very hard.'

'It is not violence that best defeats hate. The good try to love their enemies and wish them well.'

'Then I ought to love Mrs Reed and her son John, which is impossible.'

In her turn, Helen asked me to explain, and I poured out the story of my past sufferings. She heard me patiently to the end, but said nothing.

'Well,' I asked, 'is not Mrs Reed a bad, hard-hearted woman?'

'She has been unkind to you, no doubt, but wouldn't you be happier if you tried to forget her severity? Life appears to me to be too short to be spent in remembering past injustices.'

I saw by Helen's look that she no longer wished to talk, but rather to be left with her thoughts. This, though, was not allowed for long. A great rough girl came up, shouting:

'Helen Burns, if you don't go and tidy your drawer now this minute, I'll tell Miss Scatcherd to come and look at it!'

Helen got up and obeyed without delay.

Chapter 8   A Child's Shame

One afternoon when I had been at Lowood for about three weeks, I was sitting puzzling over some sums. Suddenly the whole school, including the teachers, rose, and I saw standing beside Miss Temple the same black pillar that had looked at me so severely in the breakfast room at Gateshead.

All this time I had been fearing the coming of Mr

Brocklehurst and the carrying out of his promise to Mrs Reed. Now he was speaking in a low voice to the head teacher.

'I wish the woollen socks to be looked after better. When I was here last, I examined the clothes hanging out to dry. There were many large holes in the socks. They should be mended immediately and well.'

'Your directions shall be attended to, sir,' said Miss Temple.

'And,' he continued, 'I find that some of the girls have two clean collars in a single week. It is too much. The rule limits them to one.'

'I think I can explain how that happened, sir. Two of the pupils were invited to go to tea with some friends last Thursday, and I gave them permission to put on clean collars for the occasion.'

'Well, for once it may be allowed, but please do not let it happen too often. And there is another thing which surprised me. I find, in looking at the accounts with the housekeeper, that a meal of bread and cheese has been served out to the girls during the last month. How is this? No such meal is mentioned in the school rules. Who introduced this change? And on whose orders?'

'I must be responsible for the action, sir,' replied Miss Temple. 'The breakfast was so badly cooked that the pupils could not possibly eat it. I dared not allow them to remain without food until dinner time.'

'Madam, you know that my plan in bringing up these girls is not to make them used to habits of rich living. If there should be any little accidental spoiling of a meal, they should be encouraged to suffer hunger without complaint.'

Miss Temple looked straight in front of her. Her face showed nothing of her feelings. At the same time Mr Brocklehurst, with his hands behind his back, let his eyes travel over the whole school. Suddenly he closed them for a moment, as if they had met something that shocked them. Turning back to the head teacher he spoke more rapidly than before:

'Miss Temple, Miss Temple, has that girl got curled hair? Red hair, curled all over!' And he pointed with his stick. His hand shook as he did so.

'Julia's hair curls naturally,' replied Miss Temple quietly.

'I have again and again stated that I desire the girls' hair to be arranged plainly, close to the head. Miss Temple, that girl's hair must be cut off. And I see others who have far too much. Tell the whole of the first class to turn their faces to the wall.'

Miss Temple pressed her lips firmly together, as if to hide a smile that was forming there. Leaning back a little in my seat, I could see the dissatisfied looks on the girls' faces. Mr Brocklehurst examined the backs of their heads for five minutes, and then gave the order:

'All that hair must come off.'

Miss Temple seemed about to object, but she was interrupted by the arrival of three other visitors, ladies dressed in silks and furs. They ought to have come a little sooner to have heard the gentleman's remarks, since their own hair was arranged in flowing curls. These ladies were the wife and daughters of Mr Brocklehurst; they had been examining the bedrooms, and had many complaints to make to Miss Temple about those.

Until now, while watching the scene before me with the greatest interest, I had not failed to think of my personal safety. I had sat well back on my seat, and had held my book in such a manner as to hide my face. I might have escaped notice if my book had not happened to slip from my hand. It fell with a loud crash, and immediately attracted every eye to me.

'A careless girl!' said Mr Brocklehurst. 'It is the new pupil, I see. I must not forget that I have a word to say about her. Let the child come forward.'

I could not have moved by myself, but two older girls set me on my legs and pushed me towards the terrible judge.

'Fetch that chair, and place the child on it.'

It was a very high one, and I was now on a level with Mr Brocklehurst's face.

'Ladies,' he said, turning to his family, 'Miss Temple, teachers and children, you all see this girl? She is very young. Who would think that she was already a servant of the Devil? You must keep away from her. Avoid her company, do not play with her or speak to her. Teachers, you must watch her, examine carefully her words and actions. This girl, this child, is a liar!'

Now there was a pause, during which all the female Brocklehursts shook their heads and said, 'How shameful!'

Mr Brocklehurst continued.

'This I learnt from her guardian, the generous lady who brought her up as her own daughter, until she became so ungrateful that the excellent lady was forced to separate her from her own children, for fear that her bad behaviour might harm them.'

He moved towards the door with his family. Turning at the last moment, he said:

'Let her stand half an hour longer on that chair, and let no one speak to her for the rest of the day.'

There was I, who had said that I could not bear the shame of standing in the middle of the room, now publicly dishonoured. No words can describe my feelings. But just as they began to get beyond my control, Helen passed me, and, in passing, lifted her eyes to mine and smiled. In some strange way she filled me with her own courage. I kept back my tears, lifted my head, and took a firm stand on the chair.

Chapter 9 Miss Temple

Before the half-hour ended, the bell rang. School was over, and everyone went into the dining room for tea. I now dared to get down and hide in a corner. The courage that had supported me was beginning to fail, and I felt so miserable that I sank down with my face on the ground. I cried. I had meant to be so good, to do so much at Lowood, to make so many friends, to deserve respect and love. Already I had made progress in class and received praise from my teachers, and I was well liked by the other pupils and treated as an equal by those of my own age. But now all hope was over, and I could only wish to die.

Someone came close. It was Helen Burns, bringing me my coffee and bread.

'Come, eat something,' she said, but I pushed both away from me, and continued to cry loudly.

'Helen, why do you stay with a girl whom everybody believes to be a liar, and whom everyone scorns?'

'Jane, you are mistaken. Probably no one in the school either dislikes or scorns you. Many, I am sure, pity you.'

'How can they after what Mr Brocklehurst has said?'

'Mr Brocklehurst is not a god; he is not even a great and admired man. He is not much liked here. If he had shown you any special preference, you would have made enemies. As it is, most of the girls would offer you sympathy if they dared. Teachers and pupils may look coldly at you for a day or two, but there are friendly feelings in their hearts. Besides, Jane—' She paused.

'Well, Helen?'

'If all the world hated you, and believed you to be wicked, while you knew in your heart that you had done nothing wrong, you could still hold up your head.'

I was silent. Helen had calmed me. Resting my head on her

shoulder, I put my arm around her waist. We had not sat like this for long, when Miss Temple came in.

'I came on purpose to find you, Jane Eyre,' she said. 'I want you in my room, and as Helen Burns is with you, she may come too.'

We followed her into her sitting room, where she called me to her side.

'Is it all over?' she asked, looking down at my face. 'Have you cried your sorrow away?'

'I shall never do that.'

'Why?'

'Because I have been wronged, and you, and everybody else, will think that I am wicked.'

'We shall think you what you prove yourself to be, my child. Continue to behave like a good girl, and you will satisfy us.'

'Shall I, Miss Temple?'

'You will. Now, Jane, you know that when a criminal is tried, he is always allowed to speak in his own defence. You have been charged with telling lies. Defend yourself to me as well as you can. Say whatever your memory suggests to be true, but add nothing.'

Encouraged by this, I thought for a few minutes and, having planned my story carefully, I told her the history of my childhood. As I went on, I felt that she fully believed me.

In the course of the story, I mentioned that Mr Lloyd had come to see me during my illness, and when I had finished, Miss Temple looked at me for a few minutes in silence. She then said:

'I know something of Mr Lloyd. I shall write to him. If his reply is satisfactory, you shall be publicly cleared of the charges against you. To me, you are cleared now.'

She kissed me and, still keeping me by her side, where I was happy to stand, went on to address Helen Burns.

'How are you, Helen? Have you coughed much today?'

'Not quite so much, I think.'

'And the pain in your chest?'

'It is a little better.'

Miss Temple looked thoughtful for a few minutes, then rang the bell and ordered tea. Having invited Helen and me to come to the table and drink, she unlocked a cupboard and brought out a good-sized cake. She looked on with a satisfied smile as we enjoyed the food, such a rare treat for us.

After tea, she again invited us to the fire. We sat on either side of her, and I listened with respect and admiration to the conversation between her and Helen. The meal, the bright fire, the presence of her dearly loved teacher, seemed to have excited Helen and broken down her silence. Her fine features came to life, and her intelligent eyes flashed as she and Miss Temple spoke of things that I had never heard of, of nations and times in the past, of countries far away, of books and writers. What stores of knowledge they possessed! How many books they had read!

All too soon the bell rang for bedtime. No delay could be allowed. Miss Temple kissed us both, saying as she did so:

'God keep you, my children!'

About a week after these events, Miss Temple called the school together, announced that an inquiry had been made into the charges against Jane Eyre, and stated that she was most happy to be able to inform everyone that she had been completely cleared. The teachers then shook hands with me, and a murmur of pleasure ran through the rows of my companions.

With this heavy load off my mind at last, from that hour I set to work once more. I studied hard, and was rewarded with success. My memory improved, and in a few weeks I was moved to a higher class. In less than two months I was allowed to begin French and drawing. My desire to improve myself became stronger and, in spite of the hardness of my life, I would not have exchanged Lowood for all the comforts of Gateshead.

Chapter 10   Death

As spring progressed, the discomforts of Lowood lessened. The nights were not so bitterly cold, the snows melted, the sharp winds became gentler. We could now enjoy the play hour that we spent in the garden. On Thursday afternoons (half-holidays) we now went for walks, and I learnt for the first time to take pleasure in fine scenery, in the hills that enclosed our wooded valley. Trees, flowers, and the rushing streams all filled me with joy.

But although the neighbourhood was pleasant, it was unhealthy. Before May arrived, a fever had attacked the crowded schoolroom and turned the orphanage into a hospital.

Too little food and unattended colds had made most of the pupils weak, so they caught the disease easily. Forty-five out of the eighty girls lay ill at one time. Classes were broken up, rules were forgotten. The few who remained well were allowed almost unlimited freedom, because the doctor insisted on the necessity of frequent exercise to keep them in good health.

Miss Temple's whole attention was taken up by the sick. Some girls were fortunate enough to have friends and relations prepared to remove them from danger. The teachers were fully occupied in helping them to pack and leave. Many left only to die.

But I, and the rest who continued to be healthy, did what we liked and went where we liked. Mr Brocklehurst and his family never came near Lowood now. We lived for whole days out of doors.

And where, at this time, was Helen Burns? Helen Burns was ill. For some weeks she had been removed from my sight to some room upstairs. She was not, I was told, in the same part of the house as the girls with fever, since her illness was a disease of the lungs. This, I wrongly believed, was something which time and care would be sure to cure. The idea was strengthened by the fact that she once or twice came downstairs on very warm sunny afternoons, and was taken by Miss Temple into the garden, but I was not allowed to go and speak to her.

One evening the doctor appeared at an unusual hour, a sign that someone was very ill. I was outside near the front door when he left, and I ran up to the nurse who had been speaking to him.

'How is Helen Burns?'

'Very weak,' was the answer.

'What does the doctor say about her?'

'He says she'll not be here for long.'

At ordinary times I would have taken this sentence to mean only that Helen was going to her own home; I would not have suspected that it meant that she was dying. But these were not ordinary times, and I understood immediately. I experienced a shock of terror, then a strong feeling of sorrow, and then a desire, a great need to see her. I asked which room she lay in.

'She is in Miss Temple's room,' said the nurse.

'May I go and speak to her?'

'No, child.'

It was just nine o'clock, and Miss Miller was calling the pupils to go to bed. I went with the rest.

Two hours later, I rose softly and walked quietly through the building in search of Miss Temple's room. It was at the other end of the house, but I knew my way. I passed quickly by the fever room, fearing that the nurse who was sitting up all night might hear me.

Close by Miss Temple's bed stood a smaller one. I saw the shape of a body under the bedclothes. The nurse to whom I had spoken in the garden was sitting in a chair asleep. Miss Temple was not to be seen. I learnt afterwards that she had been called to the bedside of another girl. I went up to my friend.

'Helen!' I whispered softly. 'Are you awake?'

She moved slightly, and I saw her calm, pale face.

'Is it you, Jane?' she asked, in her own gentle voice.

'Oh!' I thought. 'She is not going to die. They are mistaken. She could not speak and look so calmly if she were.'

'Why have you come here, Jane? It is past 11 o'clock. I heard the clock strike a few minutes ago.'

'I came to see you, Helen. I heard you were very ill, and I could not sleep until I had spoken to you.'

'You came to say goodbye to me, then. You are just in time, probably.'

'Are you going somewhere, Helen?'

'Yes, to my last home.'

'No, no, Helen!' I stopped, in despair. While I tried to keep back my tears, Helen began to cough. After a long silence, she whispered:

'I am very happy, Jane, and when you hear them say that I am dead, you must not be sad. We must all die one day, and the illness which is removing me is gentle and gradual. My mind is at rest. I am leaving no one to cry for me. I have only a father, and he has lately remarried and will not miss me. I am going to God.'

In a little while she added:

'How comfortable I am! That last attack of coughing has tired me a little. I feel as if I could sleep. Don't leave me, Jane. I like you to be near me.'

'I'll stay with you, dear Helen. No one shall take me away.'

I lay down beside her. She kissed me, and we both soon slept. When I awoke, it was day, and Helen was dead.

Chapter 11   A Desire for Change

The fever gradually disappeared from Lowood, but not before its violence and the number of sufferers had drawn public attention to the school. Inquiries were made into the origins of the disease, and various facts became known which excited great public anger. The unhealthy position of the building, the quantity and quality of the children's food, the impure water supply, the pupils' miserable clothing and crowded living space – all these things were discovered, and the knowledge of them brought shame on Mr Brocklehurst but improvements to the school.

Several wealthy people in the area combined to pay for the building of a better orphanage in a healthier place. New rules were made, improvements in the food and clothing were introduced, and the control of the school was put into the hands of a committee. Mr Brocklehurst still remained responsible for the financial management of the school, but his activities were watched by more generous-minded gentlemen. The school, improved in these ways, became in time a truly useful place.

I remained in it for eight years. During that time my life did not change, but I was not unhappy because I was not inactive. I had the chance of an excellent education. A fondness for some of my studies, and a desire to do my best in all of them, together with a great joy in pleasing my teachers, urged me on. In time I rose to be the best girl in the top class; then for two years I became a teacher.

Miss Temple had until now continued in charge of Lowood. To her teaching I owed the better part of my education. Her friendship and company had been a comfort to me. She had been a mother, teacher and friend to me. But then she married; she left with her husband for a distant part of the country, and was lost to me.

From that day, I was no longer the same. My world had been

for some years the narrow one of Lowood, and now that seemed empty. I remembered that the real world was wide, and offered all kinds of experiences to those who had the courage to go out into it. My holidays had all been spent at Lowood, and neither Mrs Reed nor her family had ever written to me or come to see me. School rules, school duties, school habits – these were all I knew. A sudden wild desire for freedom came over me.

'What do I want?' I asked myself. 'A new place, in a new house, among new faces, in new conditions. I want this because it is the best that I can hope for. How do people get a new place? They write to friends, I suppose. I have no friends. What do other friendless people do?'

I received no immediate reply to my question. But after a night's sleep, an idea came quietly and naturally to my mind. I must advertise.

I was up very early. I had my advertisement written before the bell rang to wake the rest of the school. It read as follows:

A young lady desires to find a post in a private family where the children are under fourteen. She is experienced in teaching the usual subjects of a good English education, together with French, drawing and music.

Address: J. E., Post Office, Lowton.

After tea, I asked and was given the new head teacher's permission to go to the neighbouring town of Lowton. I went, visited a shop or two, left my letter to the newspaper at the post office, and returned home with a lighter heart.

The next week seemed long, but at last it ended and I went once more into the town. The post office was kept by an old lady with glasses.

'Are there any letters for J. E.?' I asked.

She looked at me for a moment over her glasses, then opened

a drawer. She turned over the papers in it for so long that I began to despair. At last, having held a letter for nearly five minutes in front of her glasses, she passed it to me with an inquiring and distrustful look.

'Is there only one?' I demanded.

'There are no more,' she answered.

I put it in my pocket and hurried back. Duties were waiting for me at school. I had to sit with the girls during their study hour, then it was my turn to say prayers and to see the school to bed. It was night before I was free to open my letter. It was short:

If J. E., who advertised last Thursday, possesses the experience mentioned, and if she is able to give satisfactory proof as to good character and ability, a post can be offered her where there is only one pupil, a little girl, of less than ten years of age. The salary is thirty pounds a year. J. E. is requested to reply to Mrs Fairfax, Thornfield, near Millcote.

I examined the letter for a long time. The writing was old-fashioned and rather uncertain, like that of an oldish woman. This was satisfactory; it sounded respectable. The salary mentioned was twice what I was earning at Lowood.

Next day I made known my intention to the new head teacher, and asked her to mention the matter to the committee, or to Mr Brocklehurst, and find out whether they would allow me to leave. Mr Brocklehurst said that Mrs Reed must be written to, since she was my natural guardian. A letter was therefore sent to that lady, who wrote back saying that I could do as I pleased, as she had long given up any interest in my affairs. This reply went to the committee, and at last formal permission was given to me to take a new post, and a letter describing my experience and character, signed by members of the committee, was presented to me.

I sent a copy of this letter to Mrs Fairfax, and received the lady's reply; this stated that she was satisfied, and fixed the date when I should take up my duties as governess in her house.

Chapter 12   Thornfield

I was quite alone in the world – a strange and worrying feeling for a young woman of my very limited experience.

I had left Lowton at four o'clock in the morning, and now, at eight o'clock on the same evening, I was at a hotel in Millcote, a large industrial town, waiting to be met and taken to Thornfield. The first sense of adventure had changed to feelings of fear, and all sorts of doubts were troubling me.

After half an hour, I rang the bell.

'Is there a place in this neighbourhood called Thornfield?' I asked the waiter who answered my call.

'Thornfield? I don't know. I'll inquire.' He went away, but reappeared almost immediately.

'Is your name Eyre, miss?'

'Yes.'

'There is a person waiting for you.'

A man was standing at the entrance to the hotel, and in the lamp-lit street I faintly saw a one-horse carriage.

'I suppose,' I thought, 'judging from the plainness of the servant and the carriage, Mrs Fairfax is not a very fashionable person. All the better for me. I have only once lived among fine people, and I was very miserable with them. I wonder if she lives all alone except for this little girl. I pray God that she may not be like Mrs Reed, but if she is, I am not forced to stay with her. If I am not satisfied, I can advertise again.'

The roads were muddy, and the night misty. My driver let his horse walk all the way. It was two hours before he got down and opened a pair of gates. We passed through, went slowly up a driveway and came to the long front of a house. The door was opened by a servant.

'Will you come this way?' said the girl. I followed her across a square hall and into a small but comfortable room. There was a round table by a cheerful fire, and a high-backed, old-fashioned armchair, in which sat the neatest little old lady in a black cap and a black silk dress and with a snowy white cloth tied round her waist. She was busy sewing, and a large black cat sat at her feet. A more encouraging introduction for a new governess could hardly be imagined. As I entered, the old lady got up and came forward to meet me.

'How do you do, my dear? I am afraid you have had a long journey. John drives so slowly. You must be cold: come to the fire.'

'Mrs Fairfax, I suppose?'

'Yes, you are right. Do sit down.'

She led me to her own chair, and began to remove my coat. I begged that she would not give herself so much trouble. She then ordered me a hot drink and something to eat, and went off to see that my luggage was carried to my room.

'She is treating me like a visitor,' I thought. 'This is not how I understood that governesses are treated.'

I felt rather confused at being the object of more attention than I had ever before received, and by my employer, too.

'Shall I have the pleasure of seeing Miss Fairfax tonight?'

'Miss Fairfax? Oh, you mean Miss Adèle Varens! Varens is the name of your future pupil.'

'Really! Then she is not your daughter?'

'No – I have no family. I am so glad you have come,' she continued. 'It will be quite pleasant living here now with a companion. In the winter one feels so low-spirited alone with only the servants. But I'll not keep you sitting up late tonight. It is nearly twelve now, and you have been travelling all day.'

She took her candle and, after checking that the front door was locked, led the way upstairs. Very cold air filled the dark staircase and the long passage, and I was glad to find that my own room was small, and the furniture ordinary and modern.

Chapter 13   Strange Laughter

My room the next morning looked bright and cheerful in the sunshine, with papered walls and a rug on the floor, completely unlike the plain wood and undecorated walls of Lowood. Perhaps a happier time of life was beginning for me.

I rose and dressed myself with care. Both my clothes and my features were plain, but I was neat by nature, and my black dress fitted me well.

Going downstairs, I found the hall door open, and stepped outside. It was a fine autumn morning, and stepping onto the grass, I looked up and examined the front of the house. It was three floors high, and very large.

I was enjoying the pleasant fresh air when Mrs Fairfax appeared at the door.

'What! Out already?' she said. 'I see you are an early riser. How do you like Thornfield?'

I told her that I liked it very much.

'Yes,' she said, 'it is a pretty place, but I fear it will need serious repairs unless Mr Rochester decides to come and live here all the time.'

'Mr Rochester!' I said. 'Who is he?'

'The owner of Thornfield,' she replied quietly.

'But I thought that Thornfield belonged to you.'

'To me? Oh, no, child. What an idea! I am only the housekeeper.'

'And the little girl – my pupil?'

'Mr Rochester is her guardian. He asked me to find her a governess. Here she comes, with her nurse.'

The mystery, then, was explained. This kind little woman was not a great lady, and the equality between her and me was real. I felt better pleased than ever.

As I was thinking over this information, a little girl came running up. She was perhaps seven or eight years old, with a pale face and small features, and hair falling in curls to her waist.

'Good morning, Miss Adèle,' said Mrs Fairfax. 'Come and speak to the lady who is going to teach you.'

The child came closer. 'Is that my governess?' she asked in French, pointing to me, and addressing her nurse, who answered in the same language:

'Yes, certainly.'

'Are they foreigners?' I inquired.

'The nurse is a foreigner, and Adèle was born in Paris, and, I believe, never left it until six months ago. When she first came here she could speak no English, but now she can speak it a little.'

Fortunately I had had the advantage of being taught French by a French lady, and had practised conversation with her as often as I could. I addressed my pupil in her own language immediately and she was soon talking happily to me at the breakfast table.

After the meal, Adèle and I went to the library, which Mr Rochester had ordered to be used as the schoolroom. I found my pupil obedient, but not used to regular study of any kind. I felt it would be unwise to be too strict with her at first, so when I had persuaded her to learn a little, and it was near midday, I allowed her to return to her nurse.

As I was going upstairs, Mrs Fairfax spoke to me from across the hall:

'Your morning hours of school are over, I suppose.'

I went into the room that she was tidying.

'What a beautiful room!' I cried, as I looked round.

'Yes, this is the dining room. I have just opened the windows to let in a little air and sunshine. Everything gets so unpleasant in rooms that are rarely used.'

'What good order you keep these rooms in, Mrs Fairfax!'

'Well, Miss Eyre, though Mr Rochester's visits here are rare, they are always sudden and unexpected, and he dislikes not finding everything ready to receive him.'

'Is Mr Rochester hard to please?'

'Not particularly, but he has a gentleman's tastes and habits.'

'But has he no unusual qualities?'

'He is rather unusual, perhaps. He has travelled a great deal, and seen much of the world. I suppose he is clever, but I have never had a long conversation with him. It is not easy to describe, but you cannot be sure, when he speaks to you, whether he is joking or serious. You don't thoroughly understand him, in short – at least, I don't. But that is of no importance, he is a very good master.'

This was all the account that I got from Mrs Fairfax of her employer and mine.

When we left the dining room, she suggested showing me over the rest of the house, and I followed her upstairs and downstairs, admiring as I went. The large front rooms I thought especially grand, and some of the third-floor rooms, though dark and low, contained some interesting old furniture.

'Do the servants sleep in these rooms?' I asked.

'No, they live in a set of smaller rooms at the back.'

'You have no ghost here, I suppose?'

'None that I ever heard of,' replied Mrs Fairfax, smiling. 'Will you come and see the view from the roof?'

I followed her up a narrow staircase and a ladder. As I looked down, the area lay beneath me like a map: garden, fields, woods, the church at the gates, the road, the village, and the quiet hills.

While I turned from the scene and moved down the ladder

and the staircase, Mrs Fairfax stayed behind for a moment to lock the door leading to the roof. I reached the top floor, and waited in the long passage separating the front and the back rooms. It was narrow, low, and dark, with only one window at the far end.

As I walked on softly, I heard a most unexpected sound in so still a place – a laugh. It was a strange laugh: clear, unnatural, not at all happy. I stood still. The sound stopped, but only for a moment. Then it began again, more loudly. It ended in a noisy burst that seemed to repeat itself in every lonely room.

'Mrs Fairfax!' I called out, as I now heard her coming down the stairs. 'Did you hear that loud laugh? Who is it?'

'Some of the servants, very likely,' she answered. 'Perhaps Grace Poole. She sews in one of these rooms. Sometimes another servant is with her; they frequently get rather noisy in each other's company.'

The laugh was repeated on its low note, and ended in a strange murmur.

'Grace!' called Mrs Fairfax.

I really did not expect anyone to answer, because the laugh was so despairing and ghostlike. But the door nearest to me opened, and a servant came out – a woman between thirty and forty, with a square figure, and a hard, plain face. No more ordinary person could be imagined.

'Too much noise, Grace,' said Mrs Fairfax. 'Remember your orders!' Grace disappeared obediently, and we went downstairs to dinner.

Chapter 14   Meeting with a Stranger

The untroubled life which my first calm introduction to Thornfield seemed to promise became a reality. Mrs Fairfax remained kind and friendly. My pupil was an active, restless child, rather spoilt, but she soon became obedient and prepared to learn, and she made progress.

October, November, December passed away. On one afternoon in January, Adèle was given a holiday because she had a cold. It was a fine, calm day. Mrs Fairfax had just written a letter which was waiting to be posted, so I offered to carry it to the village, two miles away.

The ground was frozen hard, the air was still, my road was lonely. I walked fast until I became warm, then slowly to enjoy the pleasure of the hour and of the country scene. The track sloped uphill and, having walked about halfway, I sat down on a stile which led to a field. From my seat I could look down on Thornfield, whose woods climbed towards the west. The sun went down as I watched, and I turned to the east.

On the hilltop above me sat the rising moon, still pale as a cloud, but brightening from one moment to the next. In the unbroken silence I could plainly hear faint sounds of life in the distant village. I could hear, too, the flow of many little streams in the hills and valleys.

A loud noise broke in on these murmurings: a sound of heavy metallic steps on the bridge. A horse was coming: it was still hidden by a bend in the track, but it was close now. I was just leaving the stile; as the path was narrow, though, I sat still to let the horse go by. All sorts of thoughts, bright and dark, came into my mind, including troubling memories of nursery stories. I remembered some of Bessie's stories of a ghost which took the form of a horse or dog and was seen in lonely places.

The horse was very near, but not yet in sight, when I heard a movement in the bushes, and a great dog with a black and white coat ran by. It was a lion-like creature with long hair and a huge head. The horse followed – a tall animal with a rider on its back. He passed, and I went on a few steps, then I turned. The sound of something falling had suddenly attracted my attention. Man and horse were down; they had slipped on a sheet of ice. The dog came running back and, seeing his master in difficulty, came to me for help. I walked down to the traveller, who was by this time struggling to free himself from his horse.

'Are you injured, sir?'

I think he was swearing. At any rate, he did not reply directly.

'Can I do anything?' I asked again.

'You must just stand to one side,' he answered as he rose, first to his knees, then to his feet. The horse was raised, the dog silenced with the command, 'Down, Pilot!' The traveller now, bending down, felt his boot and leg, then sat down on the stile from which I had just risen.

'If you are hurt and want help, sir, I can get someone from Thornfield Hall.'

'Thank you. I have no broken bones.' He stood up again, but with a cry of pain.

A little daylight remained, and the moon was brightening. I could see him clearly. He wore a riding coat with a fur collar. He had a dark face, with severe features, a heavy forehead and eyes which were angry just now. He was past youth, but had not yet reached middle age. I felt no fear of him, and little awkwardness. If he had been a good-looking young gentleman, if he had smiled and refused my offer cheerfully and with thanks, I would have gone on my way, but the roughness of the traveller relaxed me. So when he waved me to go, I remained where I was, saying:

'I cannot think of leaving you, sir, at so late an hour, in this lonely place, until I see that you are fit to get on your horse.'

He looked directly at me for the first time.

'I should think you ought to be at home yourself,' he said. 'Where do you come from?'

'From just below.'

'You live just below – do you mean at that house?' He pointed at Thornfield Hall.

'Yes, sir.'

'Whose house is it?'

'Mr Rochester's.'

'Do you know Mr Rochester?'

'No, I have never seen him.'

'You are not a servant at the Hall, of course. You are—' He stopped, looked at my simple dress, and seemed puzzled.

'I am the governess.'

'Ah, the governess!' he repeated. 'I had forgotten.' In two minutes he rose from the stile. His face expressed pain as he tried to move.

'You may help me a little,' he said, 'if you will be so kind. I must beg you to come here.'

I came. 'Excuse me,' he continued. 'Necessity forces me to make use of you.' He laid a heavy hand on my shoulder and, leaning on me with some force, moved towards his horse. Having caught it, he mastered it immediately, and jumped onto its back.

'Now,' he said, 'just hand me my whip: it is over by those bushes.'

I found it.

'Thank you. Now get home as fast as you can.'

A touch of his heel, and horse, dog and man had disappeared down the hill.

I walked on to the village with my letter, a little excited. It was a small event, but it marked with change one hour of my dull life.

I did not like reentering Thornfield. To pass inside was to pass into too quiet an existence. For some time I remained in the garden. The clock struck, and I went in.

The hall was not dark as usual. A warm light came from the dining room, and through the open door I could see a bright fire. I heard a murmur of voices, and saw a group near the fireplace.

I hurried to Mrs Fairfax's room, but I found no candle and no Mrs Fairfax. Instead, all alone on the rug in front of the fire, I recognized the large black and white dog. It got up and came to me. I rang the bell, since I wanted a candle, and a servant entered.

'Whose dog is this?'

'He came with master.'

'With whom?'

'With master – with Mr Rochester – he has just arrived.'

'Really! Is Mrs Fairfax with him?'

'Yes, and Miss Adèle. They are in the dining room, and John has gone for a doctor, because master has had an accident. His horse fell.'

Chapter 15   Mr Rochester

For several days I saw little of Mr Rochester. In the mornings he seemed concerned with business, and in the afternoon gentlemen from the neighbourhood called and sometimes stayed to have dinner with him. When his foot was well enough, he rode out a good deal.

During this time, he rarely sent even for Adèle, and all my knowledge of him was limited to an occasional meeting around the house, when he sometimes passed me coldly, and sometimes smiled. His changes of manner did not offend me, because I saw that I had nothing to do with the cause of them.

One day after dinner a message came that Adèle and I should go downstairs. We did so, with Adèle wondering whether the little box that she had been promised had come at last. She was not disappointed. It stood on the dining-room table.

'My box of presents!' she cried, running towards it.

'Yes, there is the box. Take it into a corner and amuse yourself,' said the deep and rather scornful voice of Mr Rochester. 'And keep quiet, do you understand?'

Adèle had already seized her package.

'Is Miss Eyre there?' the master now demanded, half rising from his seat to look round. 'Come forward, and be seated here.' He pulled a chair near to his own.

'I am not fond of children's talk,' he continued. 'Don't move that chair further back. Sit down exactly where I placed it – if you please, I mean. I forget these politenesses. And I do not much care for simple-minded old ladies. I must invite mine in, though, I suppose.'

He rang the bell for Mrs Fairfax, and asked her to talk to Adèle.

Mr Rochester, as he sat in his armchair, looked not quite so severe and much less low-spirited. There was a smile on his lips, and his eyes were bright, probably with wine.

He had been looking for two minutes at the fire, and I had been looking for the same length of time at him, when, turning suddenly, he caught my eyes fixed on his face.

'You examine me, Miss Eyre. Do you think I am good-looking?'

The answer somehow slipped from my tongue before I realized it:

'No, sir.'

'Ah! Certainly there is something unusual about you!' he said. 'You have the appearance of a religious woman, quiet, simple, serious – but when one asks you a question, you have a sharp answer ready. What do you mean by it?'

'Sir, I spoke too freely. I beg your pardon. I ought to have replied that not all tastes are the same, that beauty is not important, or something of that sort.'

'You ought to have replied no such thing. Beauty not important! Go on! What fault do you find with me, may I ask?'

'Mr Rochester, I made a mistake.'

'Well, you shall pay for it. Criticize me. Does my forehead not please you? Am I stupid?'

'Far from it, sir. You would, perhaps, think me rude if I inquired in return whether you are a kind-hearted man?'

'Another sharp answer! No, young lady, I am not – not in general: but deep-down . . . perhaps. When I was as old as you I once had a certain gentleness of heart. But life has knocked me about since then, and now I am hard – except, perhaps, in one or two small places. Would you say that there was any hope for me?'

I did not know what answer to make.

'You look very puzzled, Miss Eyre. Although you are not pretty, any more than I am good-looking, a puzzled expression suits you. Besides, it is convenient, as it keeps those searching eyes of yours away from my face. Young lady, I feel conversational tonight. That is why I sent for you. It would please me now to learn more about you – therefore, speak.'

I sat and said nothing.

'You are silent, Miss Eyre.' He bent his head and looked at my face. 'Ah! You are annoyed. Miss Eyre, I beg your pardon. I expressed myself in an unfortunate manner. I desire that you will have the goodness to talk to me a little now.'

'I am happy to amuse you if I can, sir, but how do I know what subject will interest you? Ask me questions, and I will do my best to answer them.'

'Then, in the first place, do you agree that I have the right to be a little commanding, as I am old enough to be your father and have had a wide experience of life?'

'I don't think, sir, that you have a right to command me for such a reason. Your claim to such an advantage depends on the use that you have made of your time.'

'That would never suit my case, since I have made bad use of it. But will you still agree to receive my orders now and then, without being hurt by the voice of command?'

I smiled.

'The smile is a great improvement,' he said, catching the

passing expression, 'but speak, too.'

'I was thinking, sir, that very few masters would trouble themselves to inquire whether they hurt the feelings of those whom they paid for their services.'

'Ah! I had forgotten! I pay for your services! Well, for that reason, will you allow me to be a little commanding?'

'No, sir, not for that reason. But because you did forget it, and because you care about the feelings of those whom you employ, I agree to your request.'

'I shake hands with you for your answer. Not three out of three thousand schoolgirl-governesses would have replied as you have done. I don't mean to praise you: if you are different from others, it is through no goodness of your own − Nature is responsible. And then, I don't know you well. You may have unbearable faults as well as your few good points.'

'And so may you,' I thought. My eye met his as the idea passed through my mind. He seemed to read the look.

'You are right,' he said. 'I have plenty of faults. My past is not blameless. I was put on the wrong path when I was twenty-one, and have never got back to the right one since. I wish I had your peace of mind, your pure memories.'

'It is never too late to mend things, sir.'

'What is the use of thinking of it? As happiness is forbidden to me, I have a right to find pleasure in life.'

'It will taste bitter, sir.'

'Do you never laugh, Miss Eyre? Don't trouble to answer − I see that you laugh rarely, though you could be naturally joyful. You control your features, and you fear, in the presence of a man, to smile too cheerfully, speak too freely, or move too quickly. But I think you will learn to be natural with me. I see at times the look of a strange sort of bird through the close-set bars of a cage.'

I moved to rise.

'You are going now?'

'It has struck nine, sir.'

'Never mind, wait a minute. Adèle is not ready to go to bed yet. I have been watching her. About ten minutes ago she pulled out of her box a little pink silk dress. Joy lit up her face, and she rushed off to try it on. Soon she will return, looking exactly like her mother.'

Before long, Adèle's little feet were heard crossing the hall. She entered, dancing.

'Doesn't my dress look nice?' she cried, in French. 'And my shoes?'

Mr Rochester looked at her with scorn.

'Some day I'll explain her story,' he said. 'Good night.'

Chapter 16　Fire!

Mr Rochester did, on a future occasion, explain Adèle's story. One afternoon I was with her in the garden, and while she played with the dog Pilot, he asked me to walk up and down a long path in sight of her.

He told me that she was the daughter of a French dancer, whom he had once loved but who had deceived him. The dancer had run away to Italy with a musician, and he had taken pity on this child that she had left behind.

The secret he shared with me seemed a mark of respect, and I accepted it as such. His manner towards me had for several weeks been less changeable. He did not have moments of coldness. When he met me unexpectedly, the meeting seemed to give him pleasure, and he always had a word and a smile for me. When I was sent for to his presence by formal invitation, I was honoured with a warm welcome. I talked very little, but I enjoyed his conversation and his knowledge of the world.

His relaxed manner and his friendliness made me like him, and

I felt at times as if he were my relation rather than my master. He was still commanding sometimes but I did not mind this – I saw that it was his way. I became so happy with this new interest added to my life that I no longer wished for relations, and my health improved.

And was Mr Rochester now ugly in my eyes? No. Grateful feelings had made his face the object that I most liked to see, and his presence in a room was more cheering than the brightest fire. I still recognized his faults, but it seemed to me that the angry look that sometimes came over his face was a memory of some wrong done to him in the past, and I was sorry for him.

I was thinking about all this one night as I prepared myself for bed. I lay down, but could not rest. I was turning over in my mind the fact that he had told me he hated Thornfield. According to Mrs Fairfax, he rarely stayed more than two weeks at a time, but he had now remained for two months. The house would seem empty without him.

I hardly know whether I slept or not after these thoughts, but I became wide awake on hearing a faint murmur, strange and low, which sounded, I thought, just above me. I sat up in bed, listening. The sound died away.

I tried again to sleep, but my heart beat anxiously. The clock, far down in the hall, struck two. Just then it seemed that the door to my room was touched, as if fingers had passed over the wood in feeling a way along the dark passage outside. I said: 'Who is there?' Nothing answered. I became cold with fear.

Suddenly I remembered that it might be Pilot, who, when the kitchen door chanced to be left open, sometimes found his way up to Mr Rochester's room. The idea calmed me a little, and I lay down; since there was now an unbroken silence, I began to feel the return of sleep.

A dream was just coming to me, when there was a low, deep, evil laugh – the laugh of a lost spirit, so it seemed – right at the keyhole of my door. The sound was repeated. My first idea was to rise and lock my door; my next to cry out: 'Who is there?'

Something groaned. Footsteps moved away up the passage towards the top-floor staircase. A door had recently been made to close the entrance of that staircase; I heard it open and shut, and all was still.

Was that Grace Poole? It was impossible now to remain by myself. I had to go to Mrs Fairfax. I dressed, unlocked the door with a trembling hand, and opened it. To my surprise, there was a candle on the floor outside, and I was even more surprised to notice that the air was quite thick, as if filled with smoke. I became conscious of a strong smell of burning.

Something moved. It was a door left open. It was Mr Rochester's door, and the smoke rushed out from it in a cloud. I thought no more of Grace Poole, or of the laugh. In a second, I was in the bedroom. Tongues of flame were moving round the bed. The curtains were on fire. Mr Rochester lay still, in a deep sleep.

'Wake up! Wake up!' I cried. I shook him, but he only murmured and turned; the smoke had made him half-unconscious. Not a moment could be lost. I rushed to his bowl which, fortunately, was filled with water. I lifted it with difficulty, flooded the bed and the sleeper, flew back into my own room, brought my own bowl of water, and with God's help succeeded in putting out the flames.

Mr Rochester woke at last, and I heard him swear at finding himself in a pool of water.

'Is there a flood?' he asked.

'No, sir,' I answered. 'But there has been a fire. Get up, do; it is out now.'

'Is that Jane Eyre?' he demanded. 'What have you done with me? Did you plan to drown me?'

'Someone has planned something. You cannot find out too

soon who and what it is.'

He searched for dry clothes, while I brought the candle which still remained in the passage. He took it from my hand, held it up, and examined the bed, all blackened and burnt, the wet sheets and the rug all around it swimming in water. I described in a few words what had happened.

He listened very seriously. His face expressed more concern than surprise, and he did not speak immediately when I had finished.

'Shall I call Mrs Fairfax?' I asked.

'Mrs Fairfax? No, what do you want to call her for? Let her sleep in peace.'

'Then I will fetch the servants.'

'Not at all. Just be still. Take my coat, sit down in the armchair, and keep your feet out of the wet. I am going to pay a visit to the top floor. I shall take the candle. Remain where you are. Don't move, remember, or call anyone.'

He went. I watched the light disappear as he moved softly along the passage. A very long time passed. I became tired. It was cold, and I did not see the use of staying. At last he reentered, pale and low-spirited.

'I have found out what happened,' he said, setting his candle down. 'It is as I thought.'

'How, sir?'

He made no reply, but stood looking at the ground. At the end of a few minutes, he inquired in a rather strange voice:

'I forget whether you said you saw anything when you opened your door.'

'No, sir, only the candle outside.'

'But you heard a strange laugh? You have heard that laugh before, I should think, or something like it?'

'Yes, sir. There is a woman who sews here, called Grace Poole – she laughs in that way. She is a strange person.'

'That's right, Grace Poole – you have guessed it. Well, I shall think over the matter. Say nothing: I will think up some excuse for this state of affairs' – pointing to the bed – 'and now return to your own room.'

'Good night, then, sir.'

'What? Are you leaving me already?'

'You said I could go, sir.'

'But not without some thanks, when you have saved my life. At least shake hands.'

He held out his hand. I gave him mine. He took it first in one, then in both his own.

'You saved my life. I have pleasure in owing you so great a debt. I could not bear to owe it to anyone else in the world.'

He paused and looked at me. Words trembled on his lips – then he controlled himself.

'There is no debt, sir.'

'I knew,' he continued, 'that you would do me good in some way. I saw it in your eyes when I first met you. Their expression and their smile did not' – again he stopped – 'did not' – he went on quickly – 'bring such joy into my heart for nothing. Thank you for saving me. Good night!'

There was a strange energy in his voice, a strange fire in his look.

'I am only glad that I was awake,' I said, and then I prepared to leave the room.

'What! You *will* go?'

'I am cold, sir.'

'Cold? Yes, and standing in a pool. Go then, Jane, go!' But he still kept my hand and I could not free it. I thought of an excuse.

'I think I can hear Mrs Fairfax moving, sir.'

'Well, leave me.' He relaxed his fingers, and I went.

I returned to my bed, but never thought of sleep. My mind was a mixture of happiness and anxiety, judgment struggling against passion. Too feverish to rest, I rose as soon as day came.

Chapter 17   Grace Poole

I both wished and feared to see Mr Rochester on the day which followed this sleepless night. The morning, though, passed just as usual; nothing happened to interrupt the course of Adèle's quiet studies. Soon after breakfast I heard servants busy near Mr Rochester's bedroom. When I passed it later on I saw that everything was once again in complete order. A woman was sitting on a chair by the bedside, sewing rings on new curtains. It was Grace Poole.

There she sat, busy at her work, with her hard face and her ordinary-looking features, not in the least like a woman who had attempted murder and been discovered. She looked up as I was watching her, and said, 'Good morning, miss,' in her usual manner. No movement, no change of colour in her face gave any sign of feeling, of consciousness of guilt, or of fear that she might be found out.

'I will test her in some way,' I thought.

'Good morning, Grace,' I said out loud. 'Has anything happened here? I thought I heard the servants all talking together a short time ago.'

'Only that master was reading in bed last night, and fell asleep with his candle lit, and the curtains caught fire. Fortunately he woke in time and put it out.'

'A strange affair!' I said, in a low voice. Then, 'Did Mr Rochester wake nobody?'

She raised her eyes to me, and seemed to examine me carefully. Then she answered:

'The servants sleep so far off, you know, miss, that they would not be likely to hear. Mrs Fairfax's room and yours are nearest to master's. Mrs Fairfax says she heard nothing. When people are getting old they often sleep heavily.' She paused, and then added, with an appearance of carelessness:

'But you are young, miss, and perhaps a light sleeper. Did you hear a noise?'

'I did,' I said quietly. 'At first I thought it was Pilot, but Pilot cannot laugh, and I am certain that I heard a laugh, and a strange one.'

She threaded her needle with a steady hand, and then remarked calmly:

'It is hardly likely that master would laugh, miss, when he was in danger. You must have been dreaming.'

'I was not dreaming,' I replied. Again she looked at me.

'Have you told master that you heard a laugh?' she inquired.

'I have not had the opportunity of speaking to him this morning.'

'You did not think of opening your door and looking out?'

'Quite the opposite,' I said. 'I locked my door.'

'Then you are not in the habit of locking your door every night?'

The idea suggested itself to me that if she discovered that I knew of, or suspected, her guilt, she might start playing some of her evil tricks on me. Perhaps she was trying to find out my habits. I replied sharply:

'In future I shall take good care to lock everything before I lie down.'

'It would be wise to do so,' was her answer.

I hardly heard Mrs Fairfax's account of the fire during dinner. I was too busy puzzling over the mysterious character of Grace Poole, and still more over her position at Thornfield, and the reason why she had not been handed over to the law, or at least dismissed from service. Mr Rochester had admitted her guilt, but had made me swear to keep the secret. It was strange that a proud, strong-willed gentleman should be in the power of one of his own servants.

I waited impatiently for the hour when I would see Mr Rochester that evening. I had many things to say to him. I wanted to introduce the subject of Grace Poole, and hear what he would answer.

At last a servant made her appearance, but it was only to say that tea was ready in Mrs Fairfax's room.

'You must want your tea,' said the good lady, as I joined her. 'You ate so little at dinner. I am afraid you are not well today. You look feverish.'

'Oh, I am quite well!'

'Mr Rochester has had a favourable day for his journey,' she went on.

'Journey! Has Mr Rochester gone somewhere?'

'Oh, he set out the moment he had breakfasted. He has gone to the Leas, Mr Eshton's house, ten miles on the other side of Millcote. I believe there is quite a party meeting there.'

'Do you expect him back tonight?'

'No. I should think he is very likely to stay a week or more. Mr Rochester is so entertaining and so full of high spirits in society that I believe he is popular everywhere. The ladies are very fond of him.'

'Are there ladies at the Leas?'

'There are Mrs Eshton and her daughters – very fashionable young ladies, and there are the Misses Blanche and Mary Ingram, most beautiful women. When Blanche was here at a Christmas entertainment, she was considered the beauty of the evening.'

'What was she like?'

'Tall, with a long, graceful neck, strong features, large black eyes as bright as her jewels, and a fine head of black curly hair.'

'She was greatly admired, of course?'

'Yes, and not only for her beauty, but also for her skills. She sings. She and Mr Rochester sang together.'

'I did not know that Mr Rochester could sing.'

'Oh, he has a fine voice, and an excellent taste in music. He thinks very highly of Miss Ingram's singing.'

'And this beautiful and skilled lady is not yet married?'

'I believe that neither she nor her sister have very large fortunes.'

When I was once more alone, I thought about the information that I had received. I looked into my heart, examined its thoughts and feelings, and tried to bring them back to common sense. I addressed myself with severity:

'No more stupid woman than you, Jane Eyre, ever breathed the breath of life. Mr Rochester have feelings for *you*? Are you of importance to him in any way? Go! Your stupidity disgusts me. The attentions paid to a woman by her employer mean nothing to him. It is madness to let a secret love take fire within you.

'Listen, then, Jane Eyre, to your punishment. Tomorrow, place the mirror in front of you, and draw exactly what you see, without softening one fault. Write under it: "Picture of a governess, poor and plain."

'Afterwards, draw the most beautiful face that you can imagine, and paint it in your softest colours, according to the description given by Mrs Fairfax. Call it: "Blanche, a lady of rank and many skills."

'Whenever, in future, you should chance to suppose that Mr Rochester thinks well of you, take out the two pictures and compare them.'

I did so, and before long I had reason to feel satisfied with myself – with the order which I had forced on my feelings.

Chapter 18   Visitors

Mr Rochester had been absent for more than two weeks when Mrs Fairfax received a letter from him.

While she opened the envelope and read, I went on drinking my coffee. My hand shook, and half the liquid from my cup ran out onto the table.

'Well, I sometimes think we are too quiet, but now we are going to be busy enough for a little time at least,' she said. 'Mr Rochester will be here in three days' time, and a great many fine people are coming with him. He sends orders for the whole house to be prepared.'

Mrs Fairfax finished her breakfast, and hurried away to begin operations.

The next three days were certainly busy ones. I never saw such washing, brushing, beating of rugs, polishing of glasses, taking down and putting up of pictures. Adèle ran quite wild in the middle of it, dancing around the house, and looking over her dresses. She was excused from school duties because Mrs Fairfax asked for my help, and I spent each day in the kitchen helping her and the cook. I had no time for dark thoughts, and I was as active and cheerful as anyone. I lost my good temper only when I chanced to see the top-floor staircase door open and Grace Poole come down, as was her custom, to eat her dinner in the kitchen.

The strangest thing of all was that no one in the house, except me, seemed to notice her habits or wonder about them. No one discussed her position or employment. I did, in fact, once by accident hear part of a conversation on the subject, between two of the servants.

'She gets good wages, I suppose?'

'Yes, I wish I had as good. Not that I'm complaining about mine, but they're not one-fifth the sum that Mrs Poole receives.'

'She's good at her work, I expect.'

'Ah! She understands what she has to do. Not everyone could do her job.'

'That's true! I wonder whether the master—'

At that moment, one of them noticed me and made a sign to her companion to be careful.

'Doesn't she know?' I heard the other whisper.

The first one shook her head, and they both became silent.

The three days passed, and on the afternoon of the fourth day Mrs Fairfax dressed herself in her best black silk dress and put on her gold watch, since it was her business to receive the company.

At last wheels were heard. Four riders came rapidly up the driveway, followed by two carriages. Two of the riders were young gentlemen, the third was Mr Rochester, and the fourth, who rode by his side, was a lady.

'Miss Ingram!' cried Mrs Fairfax, and she hurried towards them.

A joyful movement was now heard in the hall. Gentlemen's deep voices and ladies' silvery notes sounded together. Clear above everything else, though not so loud, was the voice of the master of Thornfield Hall welcoming his guests.

Adèle begged to go down, and I had difficulty in making her understand that she must not do so unless she was sent for. I told her stories for as long as she would listen to them, then, for a change, took her out to look down the stairs and watch the servants passing backwards and forwards. Later in the evening, there was a sound of music from the sitting room, followed by conversation. I listened for a long time. Suddenly I realized that I was trying to catch the voice of my master, and to understand what he was saying.

The next day, Mrs Fairfax said to me:

'I happened to remark to Mr Rochester how much Adèle wished to be introduced to the ladies, and he said: "Oh, let her come to the sitting room after dinner, and ask Miss Eyre to come with her."'

'He said that only from politeness. I need not go, I am sure.'

'Well, I said to him that you were unused to society and would not like appearing at such a lively party, and he replied, in his quick way: "Nonsense! If she objects, tell her it is my particular wish; and if she still refuses, say that I shall come and find her."'

'I will not give him that trouble. Will you be there, Mrs Fairfax?'

'No, I begged to be excused. I'll tell you how to avoid the awkwardness of a formal entrance. You must go into the sitting room while it is empty, before the ladies leave the dinner table. Choose your seat in any quiet corner. You need not stay long after the gentlemen come in. Just let Mr Rochester see that you are there, then slip away. Nobody will notice you.'

Chapter 19   After Dinner

I felt rather nervous as the hour of my appearance in the sitting room came closer. Adèle had been in a state of joy all day, but when the business of dressing began, she became serious. I myself quickly put on my best dress (a silvery grey one, bought for Miss Temple's wedding and never worn since) and smoothed my hair.

We found the room empty. A large fire was burning, and candles shone among the beautiful flowers on the tables.

Adèle brought a small chair to my side. Before long, she touched my knee.

'May I take one of these beautiful flowers – just as a finishing touch to my dress!'

'You think too much of your dress, Adèle, but you may have a flower.' And I took a rose and fixed it in her belt. She looked at it with satisfaction, and I turned away to hide a smile.

The curtain that divided the sitting room from the dining room was now pulled to one side, and a number of ladies entered. I stood up and greeted them. One or two bent their heads in return; the others only looked at me expressionlessly.

They scattered around the room like birds, looking at the books and flowers and talking in low but clear voices. I examined them quietly, giving most of my attention to the Ingrams. The mother, Lady Ingram, was an extremely attractive but proud-looking woman, with a hard, angry eye that reminded me of Mrs Reed. The daughters, Blanche and Mary, were both very tall. I looked with special interest, of course, at the older of the two. How similar was she to Mrs Fairfax's description and the picture of her called up by my imagination?

She was beautiful, but her face was like her mother's, only younger. She was talking to Mrs Dent, a gentle lady, in such a way as to show her own cleverness but at the same time to make the other appear stupid.

Adèle went up to the ladies and greeted them in French. Miss Blanche Ingram looked scornfully down on her, Mrs Dent kissed her, and Amy and Louisa Eshton seated her between them and spoilt her as much as she could wish.

At last coffee was brought in and the gentlemen were called. I sat in the shadows. The window-curtain half hid me.

Mr Rochester arrived. I was not looking, but I saw him enter. I tried to keep my attention on my sewing. I remembered the last time I saw him, and how close I had been to him at that moment. Now, though, how distant, how far apart we were! He took a seat at the other side of the room without looking at me.

Against my will, my eyes were drawn to his face. I compared him with his guests. He was not attractive in the normal sense, but his colourless face, square heavy forehead, deep eyes, firm mouth – all decision, energy and will-power – were full of interest to me. I had not intended to love him, but the first time I saw him again I was defeated by my feelings. He made me love him without even looking at me.

I saw Mr Rochester smile. He was talking at that moment to Louisa and Amy Eshton. I saw with surprise that they received that look calmly, but I was glad. 'He is not to them what he is to me,' I thought. 'He is not of their kind. I believe that he is of mine. Though rank and wealth separate us widely, I have something in my brain and in my heart in common with him. I have certain tastes and feelings that he understands.'

Coffee was handed round. The ladies had become more cheerful since the gentlemen had entered. The older men argued about politics while their wives listened. All were busy except Blanche Ingram, who stood alone at a table. She moved towards Mr Rochester.

'Mr Rochester, why did you take charge of a little thing like that?' She pointed to Adèle. 'Where did you get her from?'

'She was left on my hands.'

'You should have sent her to school.'

'I could not afford it. Schools are so expensive.'

'Well, I suppose you have a governess for her. I saw a person with her just now – has she gone? Oh, no! There she is still, behind the window-curtain. You pay her, of course. I should think it must be just as expensive – more so, as you have to support them both as well.'

'I have not considered the subject.'

'No, you men never do consider saving. You should hear Mama speak on the subject of governesses. Mary and I had, I should think, six or seven at least. Half of them we hated, the rest we laughed at. They were all extremely annoying – were they not, Mama?'

'My dearest, don't mention governesses. The word makes me nervous. I have suffered so much from their stupidity. I thank heaven I have finished with them.'

Mrs Dent here bent over and whispered something in her ear, reminding the lady, that one of the hated profession was present.

'Let her listen!' said Blanche's mama. 'I hope it may do her good!' Then, in a lower voice, but still loud enough for me to hear: 'I noticed her, and I see in her face all the faults of her kind.'

'Oh, Mama! Don't tire us with a description. Let us change the subject. How is your voice tonight, Mr Rochester?'

'At your service, if you command it.'

Miss Ingram seated herself with proud grace at the piano.

'Mr Rochester, now sing, and I will play for you.'

'I am all obedience.'

'Now is my time to slip away,' I thought, but the voice that began to sing held my attention. It was a fine, powerful one, into which the singer threw his own feelings, his own force. I waited until the last notes died away, and then slipped out by the side door. In crossing the hall, I noticed that my shoe was undone. I stopped to tie it.

I heard the sitting room door open. A gentleman came out. Rising quickly, I stood face to face with him. It was Mr Rochester.

'How are you?' he said.

'I am very well, sir.'

'Why did you not come and speak to me in the room?'

I thought I might have put the same question to him, but I could not speak so freely. I answered:

'I did not wish to interrupt you, as you seemed busy.'

'What have you been doing during my absence?'

'Nothing special – teaching Adèle, as usual.'

'And becoming a good deal paler than you were. What is the matter?'

'Nothing at all, sir.'

'Did you catch a cold that night when you nearly drowned me?'

'No.'

'Return to the sitting room. You are leaving too early.'

'I am tired, sir.'

He looked at me for a minute.

'And a little unhappy. What about? Tell me.'

'Nothing – nothing, sir. I am not unhappy.'

'But you are – so much so that a few more words would bring tears to your eyes. In fact, they are there now. If I had the time, I would find out what all this means. Well, tonight I will excuse you, but as long as my visitors stay, I expect you to appear in the sitting room every evening. Now go, and send the nurse for Adèle. Good night, my–' He stopped, bit his lip and quickly left me.

Chapter 20   Fortunes

Those were cheerful days at Thornfield Hall, and busy days too: how different from the first three months of uneventful stillness that I had passed under its roof! There was life everywhere, movement all day long. The sitting rooms were only quiet when the fine spring weather called the guests out into the garden.

Even when rain fell for a few days, no shadow seemed to fall on their enjoyment. Indoor amusements of various kinds filled most of the time.

One day Mr Rochester was called away to Millcote on business. The afternoon was wet, and the guests did not seem to know what to do with themselves, because if he was absent for even an hour, they seemed to lose their sense of fun.

Some of the younger ladies and gentlemen began to talk about nothing in particular. The older ones settled down to a quiet game of cards. Blanche Ingram discouraged all the efforts made to draw her into conversation, and first played some tunes on the piano. Then, having chosen a book from the library, she sank down in an armchair in an attitude of obvious boredom to pass the time reading.

It was nearly time to dress for dinner when little Adèle, who was kneeling by me on the sitting-room window seat, suddenly cried in French:

'There's Mr Rochester coming back.'

I turned, and Miss Ingram rushed forward. The others, too, looked up, because at the same time the sound of wheels and of horses' feet could be heard.

'Why is he coming home in a carriage?' said Miss Ingram. 'He went out on horseback, didn't he?'

As she said this, a gentleman stepped from the carriage in travelling dress. He was a stranger.

'How annoying!' cried Miss Ingram. 'You little monkey,' she said, addressing Adèle. 'Who put you up there in the window to give false information?' And she gave me an angry look, as if I were to blame.

Some conversation could be heard in the hall, and soon the newcomer entered. He lowered his head to Lady Ingram, judging her to be the oldest lady present.

'It appears that I have come at an awkward time, madam,' he said, 'when my friend, Mr Rochester, is away from home. But I have had a very long journey, and I hope I may be allowed to remain here until he returns.'

I soon learned that his name was Mason, and that he had only recently arrived from the West Indies, where he had first met Mr Rochester. His manner was polite, his pronunciation a little unusual. He had regular features, but his eye wandered, and his expression was both unsettled and lacking in life. He seemed an unlikely kind of friend for my master.

I was thinking about this later on after dinner, when something unexpected happened. Mr Mason, not being used to cold weather, asked for some more coal to be put on the fire. The servant who brought it stopped near Mr Eshton's chair and said something to him in a low voice.

'Tell her that she shall be punished if she does not take herself away,' replied that gentleman.

'No – stop!' interrupted Mr Dent. 'Don't send her away, Eshton. She might amuse the ladies.' And, speaking more loudly, he continued, 'Ladies, there is an old woman in the servants' hall who wishes to tell your fortunes. Would you like to see her?'

'Surely, Mr Dent,' cried Lady Ingram, 'you would not encourage such a deceiver? Dismiss her, by all means, immediately!'

'But I cannot persuade her to go away, my lady,' said the servant. 'She says she will not move until she gets permission to come in here.'

'What is she like?' inquired the Misses Eshton, both at once.

'A shockingly ugly old creature, miss, almost as black as coal.'

'So she's a real gipsy,' cried one of the young men. 'Let us have her in, of course.'

'My dear boy, what are you thinking about?' said his mother.

'I cannot possibly allow such a thing,' added Lady Ingram.

'You certainly can, Mama, – and will,' stated the voice of Blanche, as she turned round on the piano seat. 'I would like to hear my fortune told: therefore, bring the old woman in.'

'My dearest Blanche! Consider–'

'I do. And I must have her – quickly!'

The servant was still unsure.

'She looks such a rough one,' he said.

'Go!' ordered Miss Ingram, and the man went. A minute later he returned.

'She won't come in here now,' he said. 'She says I must take her into a room by herself, and then those who wish to receive any information from her must go to her one by one.'

'You see now,' began Lady Ingram, 'she is making the most of her opportunity. Be advised, my dearest–'

'Show her into the library, of course,' interrupted her daughter.

'I think I had better just look at her before any of the ladies go,' said Mr Dent.

The servant went, and returned once again.

'She says, sir, that she'll have no gentlemen, nor any ladies either,' he added, keeping himself from smiling with great difficulty, 'except the young and unmarried.'

Miss Ingram rose. 'I am going first,' she said.

'Oh, my best! Oh, my love! Wait, think what you are doing!' was her fond mother's cry, but Blanche walked out of the room without a word.

A silence followed. Lady Ingram looked despairing. Miss Mary said that she would never dare to go. Amy and Louisa laughed nervously and appeared a little frightened.

The minutes passed very slowly: 15 were counted before the library door opened again, and Miss Ingram returned to us.

Would she laugh? Would she take it as a joke? All eyes met hers eagerly. She walked stiffly to her seat and took it.

'Well, Blanche?'

'What did she say?'

'Now, now, good people,' replied Miss Ingram, 'Don't get so excited. I have seen an old woman, who has told me what fortune-tellers usually tell. My wish has been satisfied, and that's all.'

She took up a book, leant back in her chair, and refused further conversation. For half an hour she never turned a page, and her face became darker, more dissatisfied and more bitterly expressive of disappointment.

Mary Ingram, and Amy and Louisa Eshton said that they dare not go alone; but they all wished to go. After the exchange of many messages through the servant, permission was at last given for the three of them to go together.

Their visit was not so quiet as Blanche Ingram's had been. We heard nervous laughter and little cries from the library, and after about 20 minutes they burst into the room running and half frightened.

'I am sure she has strange powers!' they cried. 'She told us such things! She knows all about us!' and they sank breathless into the various seats that the gentlemen hurried to bring them.

Urged for further explanation, they said that she had told them of things which they had said and done in their childhood, and described possessions that they had at home. She had even guessed their thoughts, and had whispered in the ear of each the name of the person whom she liked best in the world.

Here the gentlemen begged hard to be given more information, but they only received shy looks and laughter in return. The older ladies tried to calm the younger, while their husbands laughed.

As I watched this scene, I heard a voice at my side. I turned and saw the servant.

'If you please, miss, the old woman says there is another unmarried young lady in the room, and swears she will not go until she has seen all of them. What shall I tell her?'

'Oh, I will go, certainly,' I answered. I was glad of the opportunity to have a look at the gipsy. I slipped out of the room unnoticed and closed the door quietly behind me.

Chapter 21   The Fortune-Teller

The library looked quiet enough as I entered it, and the gipsy – if she really were one – was seated in an armchair by the fire. She had some sort of loose red coat wrapped around her, and a wide hat tied down with a cloth around her face. She seemed to be reading from a little black book, and was murmuring the words to herself, as most old women do, while she read.

As I stood on the rug and warmed my hands, I felt as calm as ever I did in my life. The woman shut her book and looked up slowly. Her hat partly shaded her face, but I could see that it was a strange one, and that she had a great deal of untidy hair. Her eyes met mine with confidence.

'Well, and do you want your fortune told?' she said in a voice as rough as her appearance.

'I don't care, mother; you may please yourself. But I ought to warn you that I shall not believe you.'

'It's the sort of answer I expected of you. I heard it in your step when you came in.'

'Did you? You've a quick ear.'

'I have; and a quick eye and a quick brain. I need them, especially when I've people like you to deal with. Why aren't you trembling?'

'I'm not cold.'

'Why aren't you turning pale?'

'I am not sick.'

'Why don't you ask me about your future?'

'I'm not silly.'

The old woman gave a high, thin-sounding laugh and, lighting a short black pipe, began to smoke. After several minutes she raised her bent body, took the pipe from her lips, and said:

'You are cold; you are sick; and you are silly.'

'Prove it,' I replied.

'You are cold, because you are alone. You are sick, because the best of feelings, the highest and sweetest that is given to man, is kept from you. You are silly, because however much you suffer, you will make no sign to it to come closer, nor will you move one step to meet it where it waits for you.'

'You could say that to almost anyone living in my condition.'

'There is hardly anyone living in exactly your condition. Your situation is actually an unusual one: very near happiness, yes, within reach of it. The materials are all prepared, and only a movement is needed to combine them.'

'I don't understand mysteries.'

'If you wish me to speak more plainly, show me your hand.'

'And you expect some money, I suppose?'

'Of course.'

I gave her a coin. She put it in an old sock, tied it up, and brought her face close to my hand.

'It is too fine,' she said. 'I cannot read it. Besides, the future is not written in a hand. It is in the face. Kneel, and lift up your head.'

'Ah! Now you are coming to reality,' I said, as I obeyed her.

A faint flame broke from the coal and the light of the fire fell on me.

'I wonder what thoughts are busy in your heart during all the hours that you sit among the fine people over there,' she said, when she had examined me for a time.

'I feel tired often, sleepy sometimes, but rarely sad.'

'Then you have some secret hope to support you and please you with whispers of the future?'

'Not I. The most I hope is to save enough money to set up a little school of my own some day.'

'A poor food for the spirit to exist on – and, sitting in that window seat (you see, I know your habits)–'

'You have learnt them from the servants.'

74

'Ah! You think yourself sharp. Well, to tell the truth, I do know one of them – Mrs Poole–'

I jumped to my feet. 'You do, do you?' I thought. 'There is the devil in this business after all, then.'

'Don't be afraid,' continued the strange being. 'You can trust Mrs Poole. She can keep a secret. But as I was saying: sitting in the window seat, do you think of nothing but your future school? Is there not one face that you study? Or perhaps two?'

'I like to study all the faces.'

'But when a lady, young and beautiful, and of high rank, sits and smiles in the eyes of a gentleman whom you–'

'Whom I what?'

'Whom you know – and perhaps think well of.'

'I don't know the gentlemen here. I have hardly spoken to any of them.'

'Will you say that of the master of the house?'

'He is not at home.'

'And because he is away from here for a few hours, do you say then that you do not know him?'

'No, but I do not see what Mr Rochester has to do with the subject.'

'I was talking of ladies smiling into the eyes of gentlemen.'

'Mr Rochester has a right to enjoy the society of his guests.'

'Yes, Mr Rochester has sat for hours, his ear towards those lovely lips, looking grateful for the entertainment given to him.'

'Grateful! I cannot remember noticing grateful feelings in his face.'

'Noticing! You have watched him, then. What did you notice, if not grateful feelings? You have seen love, haven't you? . . . And looking into the future, you have seen him married, and his bride happy?'

'Not exactly. Your gipsy's skill is at fault sometimes.'

'What in the world have you seen, then?'

'Never mind. I came here to inquire, not to tell. Is it known that Mr Rochester is to be married?'

'Yes, to the beautiful Miss Ingram. He must love such a lovely lady, and probably she loves him, or at least his money. But I told her something about the Rochester property half an hour ago that made her look rather anxious.'

'But mother, you have told me nothing of my own fortune.'

'Yours is still doubtful. When I examined your face, one feature promised one thing, another the opposite. Chance has laid on one side a measure of happiness for you. It depends on yourself to stretch out your hand and take it: but whether you will do so is the problem I am studying. Kneel again on the rug.'

'Don't keep me long: the fire is burning me.'

'The flame shines on the eye; the eye shines gently; it looks soft and full of feeling; it smiles at my words: it is open to influence. When it smiles no longer, it is sad: it shows a heaviness of spirit resulting from loneliness. It turns from me with a scornful look: it seems to refuse to accept the truth of what I have discovered. Its pride and self-control only strengthen me in my opinion. The eye is favourable.

'As to the mouth, it enjoys laughter at times; it tends to express its owner's thoughts, but it may be silent about her feelings. It is a mouth that needs to smile and speak in answer to human love. That too is favourable.

'I can see no enemy except in the forehead, and that forehead seems to say: "I can live alone, if self-respect and conditions of life demand that I should do so. Reason sits firm and will not let the feelings burst out. The passions may burn strongly and the desires imagine all sorts of useless things, but judgment will win in every argument."

'Well said, forehead; your announcement will be respected. I have formed my plans, and in them I have attended to the advice of reason. I must find smiles, not tears. But I have said enough. So far I have kept myself under control, but more might try me beyond my strength. Rise, Miss Eyre. Leave me. The play is ended.'

Where was I? Was I awake or asleep? The old woman's voice had changed. It was now as familiar to me as my own face in a mirror. I got up, but did not go. The gipsy again made a sign to me to leave. The fire shone on her arm. It was round, not thin and old. A broad ring flashed on the little finger; I had seen it many times before.

'Well, Jane, do you know me?' asked the familiar voice.

'Only take off the red coat, sir, and then–'

'But the string is in a knot – help me.'

'Break it, sir.'

'There, then.' And Mr Rochester stepped out of his borrowed clothes.

'Now, sir, what a strange idea!'

'But well carried out, don't you think?'

'With the ladies you must have managed well.'

'But not with you?'

'You did not act the character of a gipsy with me.'

'What character did I act? My own?'

'No. I believe you have been trying to make me speak too freely. You have been talking nonsense to make me talk nonsense. It is hardly fair, sir.'

'Do you forgive me, Jane?'

'I cannot tell until I have thought about it. If, after consideration, I find that I have said nothing very silly, I shall try to forgive you, but it was not right.'

'Oh, you have been very correct – very careful, very sensible.'

I considered, and thought, on the whole, that I had. It was a comfort; but, in fact, I had been suspicious almost from the beginning of the visit. I knew that fortune-tellers did not express themselves like this seeming old woman. My mind, though, had been full of Grace Poole. I had never thought of Mr Rochester.

'Well,' he said, 'what are you thinking about? What does that calm smile mean?'

'Wonder and self-satisfaction, sir. I have your permission to go now, I suppose?'

'No, stay a moment.'

'I had better not remain long, sir. It must be nearly eleven o'clock. Oh, do you know, Mr Rochester, that a stranger has arrived here since you left this morning?'

'A stranger! I expected no one. Has he gone?'

'No. He said he had known you a long time. His name is Mason, and he comes from the West Indies; from Spanish Town in Jamaica, I think.'

Mr Rochester was standing near me. He had taken my hand, as if to lead me to a chair. As I spoke, he took my wrist violently, the smile on his face stiffened, and he breathed quickly. He repeated the words 'Mason . . . the West Indies!' several times, his face becoming, as he spoke, whiter than ashes. He hardly seemed to know what he was doing.

'Do you feel ill, sir?' I inquired.

'Jane, I've had a shock. I've had a shock, Jane!' He nearly fell.

'Oh, lean on me, sir.'

'Jane, you offered me your shoulder once before. Let me have it now.'

He sat down, and made me sit beside him.

'My little friend!' he said. 'I wish I were on a quiet island alone with you, and with trouble and anger and evil memories removed from me.'

'Can I help you, sir?'

'Fetch me, Jane, a glass of wine from the dining room.'

I went. I found the whole party at supper. I filled a wine glass and I saw Miss Ingram watch me disapprovingly as I did so; she thought I was taking it for myself.

When I returned, Mr Rochester's extreme paleness had disappeared, and he looked once more firm and serious. He took the glass from my hand, swallowed the wine, and gave the glass back to me.

'What are they doing, Jane?'

'Laughing and talking, sir.'

'They don't look severe and mysterious, as if they had heard something strange?'

'Not at all. They are very cheerful.'

'And Mason?'

'He was laughing too.'

'If all these people turned away from me in scorn, what would you do, Jane? Would you go with them?'

'I rather think not, sir. I would have more pleasure in staying with you.'

'And if they drove you out of society for supporting me?'

'I could bear that for any friend who deserves my support; as you do, I am sure.'

'Go back now into the dining room. Step quietly up to Mason and whisper in his ear that Mr Rochester has come and wishes to see him. Bring him in here, and then leave me.'

'Yes, sir.'

I obeyed. Everyone looked at me as I passed among them. I went up to Mr Mason, and did as I had been directed.

At a late hour, after I had been in bed for some time, I heard Mr Rochester's voice say:

'This way, Mason. This is your room. Good night.'

He spoke cheerfully. The happy sound of his voice set my heart at rest, and I was soon asleep.

Chapter 22   A Cry in the Night

I had forgotten to close my curtain, and when the moon, which was full and bright, came and looked at me through the window, I opened my eyes. I half rose, and raised my arm to shut out the light.

Good God! What a cry!

The night − its silence − its rest was torn by a sharp, wild sound that ran from end to end of Thornfield Hall.

My heart stood still. My arm remained outstretched. The cry died away.

It came from the top floor, above me. And above me − yes, in the room just over my head − I now heard a struggle: a murderous one, it seemed, from the noise.

A breathless voice shouted:

'Help! Help! Help!' and then: 'Rochester! Come quickly!'

A door opened. Someone ran along the passage. Above me something fell, and there was silence.

I put on some clothes, though my body shook with terror, and dared to leave my room. Door after door opened. The guests were all awake. Cries, frightened murmurs sounded everywhere. 'Oh, what is it?' . . . 'Who was hurt?' . . . 'What has happened?' . . . 'Are there robbers?' were questions heard on all sides.

'Where is Rochester?' cried Mr Dent. 'I cannot find him in his bed.'

'Here! Here!' was shouted in return. 'Be calm, all of you. I'm coming.'

The door at the end of the passage opened, and Mr Rochester walked towards us with a candle. He had come down from the top floor. One of the ladies ran to him immediately, and seized his arm: it was Miss Ingram.

'All's well! All's well!' he cried. 'It is nothing. Ladies, keep away, or I shall become dangerous.'

And he looked dangerous. His black eyes flashed. Calming himself with an effort, he added:

'A servant has had a bad dream. That is all. She's a nervous person, easily excited. She imagined that she saw a ghost, and has been taken ill with shock. Now, I must see you all back to your rooms, because, until the house is settled, she cannot be looked after.'

So, by persuasion and command, he succeeded in getting them to return to rest. I went back to my room, but I did not go to bed. Instead, I began to dress myself carefully. The sounds that I had heard after the scream, and the words that had been spoken, made me sure that it was not a servant's dream that had woken the house, and that the explanation that Mr Rochester had given was only an invention to calm his guests. I dressed so I would be ready if needed, and sat for a long time by the window.

Stillness returned. Each murmur and movement gradually died away, and in about an hour Thornfield Hall seemed asleep once again. The moon was about to set, and I thought I would lie down again, dressed as I was. As I bent to take off my shoes, a hand knocked quietly at the door.

'Are you up?' asked the voice that I expected to hear.

'Yes, sir.'

'And dressed?'

'Yes.'

'Come out, then, quietly.'

I obeyed. Mr Rochester stood in the passage holding a light.

'I want you,' he said. 'Come this way. Don't hurry, and don't make a noise.'

He moved silently along the passage and up the stairs to the top floor. I followed. He held a key in his hand and, stopping at one of the small doors, put it into the lock. He paused.

'You don't turn sick at the sight of blood?'

'I think I shall not, but I have never been tested.'

He turned the key and opened the door. I saw a room that I remembered having seen before, on the day that Mrs Fairfax showed me over the house, but now an inner door could be seen, which had been hidden then behind a curtain. This door was open, and I heard from the room beyond a wild animal-like sound, almost like a dog quarrelling. Mr Rochester, putting down his candle, said to me: 'Wait a minute,' and went forward to the inner room. A shout of laughter greeted his entrance, noisy at first, and ending in Grace Poole's ghostly: 'Ha! Ha!' She, then, was there.

In a moment my master came out and closed the door.

'Here, Jane,' he said, and I walked round to the other side of a large bed with curtains closed around it. An armchair was near the bed, and a man sat in it, dressed except for his coat. I recognized his pale and seemingly lifeless face – the stranger, Mason. I saw, too, that one side of his shirt and one arm were covered with blood.

'Hold the candle,' said Mr Rochester. I took it. He found a bowl of water, opened the shirt of the wounded man, and began to wash away the blood, which was flowing fast. Mr Mason soon opened his eyes and groaned.

'Am I in danger?' he asked.

'No – it's nothing serious. Don't worry, man! I'll fetch a doctor for you now myself. You'll be able leave by morning. Jane,' he continued.

'Sir?'

'I shall have to leave you in this room with this gentleman for an hour, or perhaps two hours. You will wash away the blood when it returns. If he feels weak, you will put a glass of water to his lips. You will not speak to him at all – and Richard, you will be risking your life if you speak to her. If you excite yourself, I cannot be responsible for what may happen.'

Again the poor man groaned. Mr Rochester watched me

carry out his directions for a moment. Then, saying, 'Remember – no conversation,' he left the room. I experienced a strange feeling as the key turned in the lock, and the sound of his steps died away.

Here I was on the top floor, locked into one of its rooms, with a pale and bloody sight under my eyes and hands, and a murderess hardly separated from me by a single door. The rest I could bear, but I trembled at the thought of Grace Poole bursting out on me.

I had to keep to my post, though. And I listened while I watched. I listened, but all night I heard only three sounds – a footstep, an animal murmur, and a deep human groan.

My own thoughts, too, worried me. What crime was this, what mystery, that broke out first in fire and then in blood, in the middle of the night? What creature was it that in an ordinary woman's shape possessed the voice of an evil spirit, or of a wild animal? And this man whom I was now bent over, this quiet stranger – how had he come to be mixed up in this affair of terror? What made him find his way to this part of the house? Why did he obey Mr Rochester's demands for secrecy? Why did Mr Rochester desire this secrecy?

'When will he come? When will he come?' I cried to myself, as the night slowly passed, while the bleeding man groaned and no help came.

Chapter 23   Daylight

The candle at last went out, and a grey light outside showed that day was coming closer. In a little while I heard the noise of Pilot far below. Hope returned.

Five minutes later, Mr Rochester entered, and with him the doctor he had been to look for.

'Now, Carter, be quick,' he said to the other. 'I can give you only half an hour for cleaning the wound, tying it up, getting him downstairs and everything.'

'But is he fit to move, sir?'

'Yes, yes. It is nothing serious. He is nervous; he needs encouragement. Come, set to work.'

He walked up to Mason.

'Now, my good man, how are you?' he asked.

'She's finished me, I fear,' was the faint reply.

'Courage! You've lost a little blood, that's all. Carter, tell him there's no danger.'

'I can do that with sincerity,' said the doctor, 'although I wish I could have got here sooner. But how is this? This wound on the shoulder was not done with a knife: there have been teeth here!'

'She bit me,' murmured Mason. 'She attacked me like a wild cat, when Rochester got the knife from her. I did not expect it; she looked so quiet at first.'

'I warned you,' was his friend's answer. 'I told you to be careful when you went near her. Besides, you could have waited until tomorrow and had me with you.'

'I thought I could have done some good.'

'You thought! You thought! Yes, it makes me impatient to hear you. Still, you have suffered for not taking my advice. Carter, hurry! Hurry! The sun will soon rise, and I must have him away from here.'

'In a minute, sir; but I must look at this other wound in the arm. She has had her teeth here, too, I think.'

'She sucked the blood. She said she'd suck it from my heart,' said Mason.

I saw a strong expression of disgust and hatred pass across Mr Rochester's face, but he only said:

'Come, be silent, Richard, and never mind her nonsense. Don't repeat it. Jane,' he continued, turning to me, 'take this key.

Go down to my bedroom, and bring a clean shirt. Then go into Mr Mason's room and find his coat.'

I obeyed. In a short time the wounded man was dressed and lifted onto his feet. By this time it was half past five. Supported by Mr Rochester and the doctor, he seemed to walk fairly easily, and was helped downstairs with as little noise as possible. Outside, a carriage was waiting.

'Take care of him,' said Mr Rochester, as Carter followed Mason into the carriage, 'and keep him at your house until he is quite well. Goodbye, Richard.'

'Rochester—'

'What is it?'

'Let her be taken care of. Let her be treated kindly. Let her—' Mason stopped, and burst into tears.

'I do my best, and have done it, and will do it,' was the answer. Mr Rochester shut the door, and the carriage drove away. 'I wish that God would put an end to all this!' he added.

He moved with slow steps towards a door in the wall bordering the kitchen garden. He opened it, and stood waiting for me.

'Jane,' he said. 'Come where there is some freshness for a few moments. That house is a prison, don't you feel?'

'To me it seems a lovely place, sir.'

'A veil of inexperience covers your eyes. Now here,' he said, pointing to the leafy area that we had entered, 'everything is real, sweet and pure.'

He wandered down a path edged with all kinds of flowers, as fresh now as a beautiful spring morning could make them. The sun was just appearing, and its light fell on the trees and the quiet walks beneath them.

'Jane, will you have a flower?'

He picked a half-open rose, the first on the bush, and offered it to me.

'You have passed a very strange night, Jane, and it has made you look pale. Were you afraid when I left you alone with Mason?'

'I was afraid of someone coming out of the inner room.'

'But I had locked the door. You were safe.'

'Will Grace Poole continue to live here, sir?'

'Oh, yes! Don't trouble yourself about her.'

'But it seems to me that your life is hardly safe while she stays.'

'Never mind. I will take care of myself.'

'Is the danger that you feared last night gone now, sir?'

'I cannot be certain until Mason is out of England, and not even then.'

'But Mr Mason seems a man who is easily influenced. Your influence, sir, is plainly strong with him. He will never purposely harm you.'

Mr Rochester laughed bitterly, quickly took my hand, and just as quickly threw it from him.

'Oh, no! He will not disobey me . . . but without intending it, he might in a moment, by one careless word, cause me to lose, if not my life, my only chance of happiness. I must keep him from finding out that harm to me is possible. Now you look puzzled, and I will puzzle you further. You are my little friend, aren't you?'

'I like to serve you, sir, and to obey you in everything that is right.'

'Exactly. I see you do. I see sincere pleasure in your face when you are helping me in what you call "everything that is right". But if I told you to do what you thought was wrong, my friend would then turn to me, quiet and pale, and would say, "No, sir, that is impossible." Well, you, too, have power over me, and may harm me, and I dare not show my weak spot, for fear that, loyal and friendly though you are, you might strike me immediately.'

'If you have no more to fear from Mr Mason than you have from me, sir, you are very safe.'

'I pray to God that it may be so! Here, Jane, is a seat. You won't refuse to take a seat by my side, will you?'

I felt that refusal might be unwise.

'Well, Jane, I'll ask your advice. Suppose you were no longer a well-brought-up young girl, but a wild boy, spoilt from childhood. Imagine yourself in a distant foreign land. Suppose that you there make a serious mistake, one whose results must follow you all through life. Remember, I don't say *crime*: my word is *mistake*. Life becomes bitter and miserable; you wander here and there, trying to find happiness in aimless pleasure. Tired and dissatisfied, you come home after many years. You meet someone different. You find, in this stranger, the good and bright qualities which you have been searching for without success for 20 years. You feel purer feelings coming back to you, and you wish to begin a new life. In order to do this, would you be right to disregard a custom which neither your sense of morality accepts nor your judgment approves? Would it be right to risk the world's opinion in order to join yourself for ever to this gentle stranger?'

He paused for an answer, and what could I say? Oh, for some good spirit to suggest a wise and satisfactory reply!

'Sir,' I answered. 'No man's improvement should depend entirely on a companion. He should look higher than his equals for strength to lead a better life.'

'But the means! God, who does the work, chooses the instrument. I believe I have found the instrument for my own cure in . . .'

He paused. The birds went on singing, and the leaves lightly moving. At last I looked up at the speaker. He was looking eagerly at me.

'Little friend,' he said, in quite a changed voice, while his face changed too, losing all its softness and becoming hard and scornful, 'you have noticed my feelings for Miss Ingram. Don't you think that if I married her, she would improve me?'

He got up and went to the far end of the path. When he came back, he was whistling a tune.

'She's a rare one, isn't she, Jane?'

'Yes, sir.'

'A real beauty, Jane. Ah, there are Dent and Lynn in the garden. Go back to the house by that side gate.'

As I went one way, he went another, and I heard him saying cheerfully to his guests:

'Mason was up before you this morning. He was gone before sunrise. I got up at four to see him go.'

Chapter 24   News from Gateshead

On the afternoon of this same day, I was called downstairs by a message that someone wanted me in Mrs Fairfax's room. There I found a man with the appearance of a gentleman's servant, and dressed in black.

'I expect you hardly remember me, miss,' he said, rising as I entered, 'but I was a coachman with Mrs Reed when you were at Gateshead, and I still live there.'

'Oh, how do you do? I remember you very well. And how is Bessie? You are married to Bessie, aren't you?'

'Yes, my wife is very well, thank you.'

'And are the family well at the house?'

'I am sorry I can't give you better news of them, miss. Mr John died a week ago in London.'

'Mr John?'

'Yes. His life was very wild. He got into debt and into prison; his mother helped him out twice, but the third time she refused, and the next news was that he was dead. They say he killed himself.'

I was silent. The news was terrible. The coachman went on:

'Mrs Reed had been in poor health herself for some time. The loss of money and fear of having none at all were troubling her. The shock of Mr John's death was too sudden. She fell ill, and remained for three days without speaking, but last Tuesday she seemed rather better, and kept making signs to Bessie and murmuring. At last my wife understood the words, "Bring Jane Eyre. I want to speak to her." She told Miss Eliza and Miss Georgiana and advised them to send for you, and at last they agreed. If you can get ready, miss, I would like to take you back with me early tomorrow morning.'

'Yes, I shall be ready. It seems to me that I ought to go.'

Having directed him to the servants' hall, I went in search of Mr Rochester. He was entertaining some of his guests. It needed some courage to interrupt the party, but my business was urgent. I walked up to my master, who stood by Miss Ingram's side. She turned as I came near and, when I said in a low voice, 'Mr Rochester', made a movement as if she wished to order me away.

Mr Rochester followed me out of the room.

'Well, Jane?' he said, as he rested his back against the schoolroom door, which he had shut.

'If you please, sir, I want permission to be absent for a week or two.'

'What for? Where are you going?'

'To see a sick lady, my uncle's wife, at Gateshead. She has sent for me.'

'And what good can you do her? Nonsense, Jane! I would never think of running hundreds of miles to see someone who will probably be dead before you reach her.'

'I cannot be easy in my mind if I ignore her wishes.'

'Promise me only to stay a week—'

'I had better not give my word. I might be forced to break it.'

'But you will come back? You will not be persuaded to remain with her for ever?'

'Oh, no! I shall certainly return if all is well.'

'Well, you must have some money. I have given you none yet. How much have you in the world, Jane?'

'A lot less than a pound, sir.'

He laughed, and searched his pockets.

'Here,' he said, offering me a fifty-pound note. I told him I had no change.

'I don't want change: you know that. Take your salary.'

I refused to accept more than he owed me, which was only fifteen.

He looked angry at first. Then, as if remembering something, he said:

'Right! Right! I had better not give you all of it now. You would, perhaps, stay away for three months. There are ten pounds: that's plenty, isn't it?'

'Yes, sir, but you now owe me five.'

'Come back for it.'

'Mr Rochester, I may as well mention another matter of business to you while I have the opportunity.'

'Matter of business? I am anxious to hear it.'

'You have informed me, sir, that you will soon be married. In that case, sir, Adèle ought to go to school.'

'To get her out of my bride's way? And you?'

'I must find other employment somewhere. I must advertise.'

'Of course!' he cried, with a sharpness of voice and a twisting of his features unusual to him. 'You dare to advertise! I wish I had only offered you a pound instead of ten. Give me back nine pounds, Jane, I've a use for it.'

'And so have I, sir,' I replied, putting my hands behind me.

'Ungenerous little thing!' he said. 'Give me five pounds, Jane.'

'No, sir, not even five pence.'

'Just let me look at the money.'

'No, sir, you are not to be trusted.'

'Jane!'

'Sir?'

'Promise me not to advertise, and to leave the finding of your employment to me.'

'I shall be glad to do so, sir, if you, in your turn, will promise me that Adèle and I shall both be safely out of the house before your bride enters it.'

'Very well! You are going tomorrow, then?'

'Yes, sir, early.'

'Then you and I must say goodbye for a little while?'

'I suppose so, sir.'

'And how do people perform that ceremony of parting? Teach me, Jane.'

'They say goodbye, or any other form that they prefer.'

'Then say it.'

'Goodbye, Mr Rochester, for the present.'

'It seems dry to me, and unfriendly. I would like something else. If we shook hands, for example; but no – that would not satisfy me either.'

'How long is he going to stand with his back against that door?' I asked myself. 'I want to begin packing.'

The dinner bell rang, and he rushed away without another word.

Chapter 25   Mrs Reed's Secret

I reached Gateshead at about five o'clock in the afternoon and went first to see Bessie, who persuaded me to have some tea. Old times crowded back into my mind as I watched her moving about in her home, giving her children an occasional light blow or push, just as she used to give me in former days. She still had her quick temper as well as her good looks.

After about an hour I walked with her towards the house which I had left in despair and loneliness nearly nine years before. My future was still doubtful, and I had an aching heart; I still felt like a wanderer on the face of the earth, but I experienced firmer trust in myself and less fear of injustice. The wound of the wrongs done to me, too, was now quite gone.

'You shall go to the breakfast room first,' said Bessie. 'The young ladies will be there.'

In another moment I was within that room. There was every piece of furniture looking just as it did on the morning when I was first introduced to Mr Brocklehurst. Even the rug that he had stood on still lay in front of the fire. Looking at the bookshelves, I thought I could see *Gulliver's Travels* in its old place on the third shelf.

The living persons, though, had changed so much that I did not recognize them. Two young ladies appeared before me. One was very tall and thin, with a severe expression and an extremely plain dress. This, I felt, must be Eliza. The other, fair-skinned, with good-looking and regular features, blue eyes and yellow hair, was Georgiana.

Both, as I entered, rose to welcome me, and then, after the greeting, paid me no further attention except that the younger one examined in a critical manner the simple and unfashionable quality of my clothes.

Their coldness no longer had any power to hurt me, and when they did not immediately suggest that I should see their mother, I went without asking them.

I did not need to be guided to the room to which I had so often been called for punishment in former days. I went to the bed, and eagerly looked at the familiar features. It is a happy thing that time ends the desire for violence, and calms the feelings of anger and hate. I bent down and kissed my aunt. She looked at me.

'Is it Jane Eyre?' she said.

'Yes, Aunt Reed. How are you, dear Aunt?'

I had once sworn never to call her Aunt again. I thought it no shame to forget this now. My fingers held her hand, which lay outside the sheet, but Mrs Reed took her hand away and turned her face from me.

I felt pain, and then I felt anger. My tears had risen, just as in childhood, but I kept them back.

'You sent for me,' I said, 'and I am here.'

'Oh, of course! Tell my daughters that I wish you to stay until I can talk to you about something that is troubling me. There was something I wished to say . . . let me see . . .'

The wandering look and strange voice told me what change had taken place in her once healthy form. Turning restlessly, she found my arm resting on a corner of the sheet.

'Sit up properly!' she said. 'Are you Jane Eyre?'

'I am Jane Eyre.'

'I have had more trouble with that child than anyone would believe. Such an unwelcome thing to be left on my hands! I was glad to get her away from the house. The fever broke out in Lowood. She did not die, but I said she did – I wish she had died!'

'Why do you hate her so, Mrs Reed?'

'I had a dislike for her mother. My husband was so fond of his sister that he sent for her baby when she died. It was a weak thing, always crying. My husband used to take more notice of it than of his own children, and he was angry with them when they refused to play with it. He made me promise to look after it. John is not like his father, and I am very glad of it. Oh, but I wish he would stop asking me for money! John spends terribly on cards, and always loses, poor boy! I have a lot of troubles. What is to be done?'

By now she was becoming very excited and confused. Bessie

with difficulty persuaded her to take some medicine. She became calmer, and I left her.

More than ten days passed before I had any more conversation with her. I had little satisfaction in the society of my two cousins, but I had my drawing materials with me, and with them I kept myself busy. Georgiana, after a time, was pleased to let me draw a picture of her, and to share with me the various love affairs that she had enjoyed in London two years before. Eliza spoke little, but occasionally quarrelled with her sister.

One wet, windy afternoon, Georgiana had fallen asleep over a book, and Eliza had gone to church. I thought I would go upstairs and see how the dying woman was; little attention was paid to her, since the servants and nurse were lazy, her daughters did not care, and Bessie was busy with her own family. I found the sickroom unattended, as I had expected.

The sick woman lay still, and I looked for a long time at the woman who could now no longer look at me. I remembered Helen Burns, and was listening in my imagination to her well-loved voice as she said her last words to me, when a weak murmur came from the bed:

'Who is that?'

I answered, but it was some time before Mrs Reed could recognize me.

'I am very ill now,' she said, after a time. 'It is better that I should tell someone what is on my mind before I die. What seems of little importance while we are healthy, troubles us in such an hour as this is to me. Is there anyone else here?'

I told her that we were alone.

'Well, I have twice done you a wrong which I am now sorry for. One was in breaking the promise which I gave to my husband to bring you up as my own child. The other . . .' She stopped. 'After all, it is of no great importance, perhaps,' she murmured to herself, 'and then I may get better, and to shame myself so to her is painful.'

She made an attempt to move, but failed. Her face changed.

'Well, I must do it. I had better tell her. Go to my writing desk, open it, and take out a letter that you will see there.'

I obeyed her directions.

'Read the letter,' she said.

It was short, and read as follows:

Madam,

Will you have the goodness to send me the address of my brother's child, Jane Eyre, and to tell me how she is? It is my intention to write soon and to ask her to come and live with me here in Madeira. God has given me success in my business, and as I am unmarried and childless, I wish to leave her at my death whatever I may then possess.

I am, Madam,

Yours truly,

JOHN EYRE.

It was dated three years back.

'Why did I never hear of this?' I asked.

'Because I disliked you too deeply. I could not forget how you once accused me of cruelty and told me you hated me more than anyone in the world. I wrote and told your uncle that Jane Eyre had died of fever at Lowood. Now do as you please.'

'Dear Mrs Reed,' I said, 'think no more of all this. Forgive me for my passionate language – I was a child then. If you could only be persuaded to think of me kindly–'

'You have a very bad nature,' she replied, 'and even now I find it impossible to understand how for nine years you could be patient under any treatment, and in the tenth break out, all fire and violence.'

'My nature is not as bad as you think. Many a time, as a little child, I would have been glad to love you if you would have let me. Kiss me, Aunt.'

I moved my face down to her lips. She would not touch it. Bessie entered and I waited half an hour longer but the sick woman made no sign. At 12 o'clock that night she died.

Chapter 26 Return to Thornfield

Mr Rochester had given me only one week's holiday, but a month passed before I left Gateshead. I wished to leave after the funeral, but my cousins urged me to stay until they had completed their own arrangements for leaving, Georgiana to her uncle's home in London, where she married soon afterwards, and Eliza to a religious house in France, where she spent the rest of her life in prayer.

My journey seemed very long, and my mind was not at rest. I was returning to Thornfield, but how long was I going to remain there? I had heard from Mrs Fairfax that the party at the Hall had ended, and that Mr Rochester had left for London, probably to make arrangements for his wedding since he talked of buying a new carriage. He was expected back soon.

I had not told Mrs Fairfax the exact date of my return, as I did not wish the carriage to meet me at Millcote. I planned to walk the distance quietly by myself, taking an old road through the fields. It was a pleasant summer evening, and the farmers were at work all along the way.

I walked on until I had only a field or two still to cross. The trees were covered in wild roses, but I had no time to pick any. I wanted to be at the house. I passed a tall bush, I saw the narrow stile with its stone steps; and I saw Mr Rochester sitting there, a book and pencil in his hand; he was writing.

For the moment I was unable to move. I had not thought I

would tremble in this way when I saw him, nor lose my voice in his presence. I wanted to go back and enter the house by another way, but I could not move. Then it was useless, because he had seen me.

'Ah!' he cried, and he put down his book and pencil. 'There you are! Come on, if you please!'

I walked towards him, doing my best to appear calm.

'And is this Jane Eyre? Have you come from Millcote, and on foot? Yes...just one of your tricks, to return quietly to your home in the half-light, as if you were a dream or a spirit. What have you been doing this last month?'

'I have been with my aunt, sir, who is dead.'

'A truly Jane-like reply! Good spirits be my guard! She comes from the other world – from the land of the dead! If I dared, I'd touch you to see if you are substance or shadow. Disloyal!' he added, when he had paused for a moment. 'Absent for a whole month, and quite forgetting me, I'll swear!'

He did not leave the stile, and I hardly liked to ask to go past him. I inquired soon whether he had been to London.

'Yes, I suppose Mrs Fairfax has told you the reason. You must see the carriage, Jane, and tell me if it won't suit Mrs Rochester exactly. I wish, Jane, that I were more of a match for her in appearance. Tell me now, can you give me some medicine to make me a good-looking man?'

'It would be beyond the power of magic, sir.' And in thought I added, 'A loving eye is all the medicine that is needed. To such an eye you are good-looking enough, or rather, your severity has a power beyond beauty.'

Mr Rochester had sometimes read my unspoken thoughts with a quickness that I did not understand. In the present case, he took no notice of my sharp words, but he smiled at me with a certain smile that he had of his own and which he used only on rare occasions. It was the real sunshine of feeling.

'Pass, Jane,' he said, making room for me to cross the stile. 'Go home, and rest.'

All I had to do now was to obey him in silence. I got over the stile without a word and meant to leave him calmly. But some force caused me to turn round, and I said, in spite of myself:

'Thank you, Mr Rochester, for your great kindness. I am strangely glad to get back again to you. Wherever you are *is* my home – my only home.'

I walked on so fast that even he could hardly have followed me if he had tried. Little Adèle was half wild with joy when she saw me. Mrs Fairfax received me with her usual plain friendliness, and even the servants smiled. This was very pleasant: it was the first time in my life that I had experienced the pleasure of coming home.

Two weeks of calm followed my return to Thornfield. Nothing was said of my master's marriage, and I saw no preparations going on for such an event. One thing especially surprised me, and that was that there were no journeyings backwards and forwards, no visits to Ingram Park. Nor could I ever remember the time when my master's face had been so cheerful. If, in the moments that I and my pupil spent with him, I looked unhappy, he became even more high-spirited. He had never called me more often to his presence, had never been kinder to me when I was with him, and ah! I had never loved him so well.

Chapter 27   The Storm Breaks

On Midsummer evening, Adèle, tired of picking wild fruit, had gone to bed early. I watched her fall asleep, and when I left her I went into the garden.

It was now the sweetest hour of the twenty-four. Sunset was

giving way to moonrise. I found a path where I could wander unseen, but it was not long before something made me pause – not a sound, not a sight, but a smell. This new smell was not that of leaf or flower. It was – I knew it well – Mr Rochester's tobacco. I saw him in the distance, and I stepped to one side to a sheltered seat. 'If I sit still,' I thought, 'he will never see me.'

He wandered around, examining the fruit on the bushes, and then bending towards a flowering plant. A great insect went noisily by me and settled near his foot. He saw it, and turned to look at it more closely.

'Now he has his back towards me,' I thought. 'Perhaps if I walk softly, I can slip away unnoticed.'

I walked gently along a grassy border, but as I crossed his shadow, thrown long over the garden by the moon, he said quietly, without turning round:

'Come back, Jane. On so beautiful a night it is a shame to remain indoors.'

It is one of my faults that though my tongue is sometimes ready enough with an answer, there are times when it fails sadly in making an excuse; and this weakness always appears at some difficult moment, when a simple word is needed to get out of an awkward situation. It failed me now.

'Jane,' he began again, as we walked, 'Thornfield is a pleasant place in summer, isn't it? Wouldn't you be sorry to leave it?'

'Must I leave, sir?' I asked.

'I am sorry, Jane, but I believe you must.'

'Then you *are* going to be married, sir?'

'In about a month I hope to bring home my bride. I have already, through her mother, heard of a place that I think will suit you. It is to educate the five daughters of a lady in the west of Ireland.'

'It is a long way away, sir.'

'Never mind. A girl of your sense will not object to the

journey or the distance. We have been good friends, Jane, haven't we?'

'Yes, sir.'

'I shall never see you again. I suppose that you will forget me?'

'That I *never* would, sir: you know...' It was impossible to continue.

'Jane, do you hear that bird singing in the wood?'

As I listened, I cried. I could hide my feelings no longer. When I did speak, it was to express a passionate wish that I had never been born, or never come to Thornfield.

The violence of my feeling, excited by grief and love, was gaining control, and demanding a right to win and to speak.

'I love Thornfield – I love it because I have lived in it a full and happy life, for a little while at least. I have not been scorned or badly treated. I have talked, face to face, with what I enjoy – with a strong and original mind. I have known you, Mr Rochester, and I find it unbearable that I must be separated from you for ever. I see the necessity for leaving, and it is like looking at the necessity of death.'

'Where do you see the necessity?'

'You, sir, have placed it in front of me, in the form of your bride.'

'My bride! I have no bride!'

'But you will have.'

'Yes! I will! I will!' He looked determined.

'Then I tell you I must go!' I replied, moved to something like passion. 'Do you think I can stay to become nothing to you? Do you think I am a machine without feelings? Do you think that, because I am poor and plain, I am soulless and heartless? You think wrong! And if God had given me some beauty and great wealth, I would have made it as hard for you to leave me as it is now for me to leave you. I am not talking to you now by the standards of custom and the world. It is my spirit that addresses your spirit, as if we stood before God, equals, as we are!'

'As we are!' repeated Mr Rochester. 'So,' he added, enclosing me in his arms. 'So, Jane!'

'Yes, so, sir,' I replied, 'but in fact not so, for you are going to marry a person who is not good enough for you – one with whom you have no sympathy and whom I do not believe that you truly love. I would scorn such a union; therefore I am better than you – let me go!'

'Where, Jane? To Ireland?'

'Yes, to Ireland. I have said what I think, and can go anywhere now.'

'Jane, be still; don't struggle so, like a wild bird.'

'I am no bird. I am a free human being with an independent will, which I am now using to leave you.'

Another effort set me free.

'And your will shall decide your future,' he said. 'I offer you my hand, my heart, and a share of all my possessions.'

I was silent. I thought he was laughing at me.

'Do you doubt me, Jane?'

'Completely.'

'You do not trust me?'

'Not a bit.'

'Am I a liar in your eyes?' he asked passionately. 'Little doubter, I will make you believe me! What love have I for Miss Ingram? None. What love has she for me? I caused a story to reach her that my fortune was not a third of what was supposed, and when I visited her to see the result, it was coldness from her and her mother. I would not – I could not – marry Miss Ingram. I have only tried to make you jealous. I love you as much as I love myself. You – poor and plain as you are – I beg you to accept me as a husband.'

I began – as a result of his seriousness and especially his plain speaking – to believe in his sincerity.

'Do you truly love me? Do you really wish me to be your wife?'

'I do. I will swear it.'

'Then I will marry you.'

He pulled me to him. 'Make my happiness – I will make yours. God forgive me! Let no man prevent me: I have her and will keep her.'

'There is no one to prevent us from marrying, sir. I have no relations to make it their business.'

'No – that is the best of it,' he said. If I had loved him less, I might have thought his voice and look of victory wild. 'I know that my God approves of what I do. For the world's judgment, I care nothing.'

But what had happened to the night? The moon was clouded over, and wind was beginning to shake the trees. A flash lit up the sky, and there was a crack, a crash.

'We must go in,' said Mr Rochester. 'The weather is changing. I could have sat with you until morning, Jane.'

The rain poured down. He hurried me to the house. He was shaking the water out of my loosened hair when Mrs Fairfax came out of her room. She looked pale, serious, and surprised. I only smiled at her and ran upstairs.

'Explanations will do for another time,' I thought.

The storm continued all night, with thunder, lightning and rain. In the morning little Adèle came running into my room to tell me that a great tree at the bottom of the garden had been struck by lightning and split in two.

Chapter 28   The Torn Veil

Our wedding was planned for a month's time. During that period, in spite of Mr Rochester's opposition, I continued to work as

Adèle's governess and refused to spend any time with him except the usual after-dinner hour. I refused, too, his offers of jewels and rich clothes, which reminded me too greatly of my lack of wealth. In this connection, I remembered what, in the speed of events, I had forgotten – the letter from my uncle, John Eyre of Madeira, to Mrs Reed, and his intention of making me his heir.

'It would certainly be satisfactory,' I thought, 'if I had even a small yearly amount of money of my own. I will write to my uncle and tell him I am alive and going to be married.' And this I immediately did.

The month passed, and its final hours arrived. All preparations for the bridal day were completed. My boxes were packed, locked, and waiting for the nailing on of the address cards, on which Mr Rochester had himself written the name 'Mrs Rochester'. Immediately after the ceremony we were going to leave for Europe.

I felt restless and excited. It was not only the hurry of preparation that made me feverish, nor the thought of the new life that would begin the next day. A third matter influenced my mind more than they did.

My mind was troubled. Something had happened which I could not understand, and no one knew of or had seen the event except myself. It had happened the night before, when Mr Rochester was absent from home on business. I waited now for his return, eager to receive from him a solution to the puzzle.

At last he came, and I found him at supper.

'Take a seat and share my meal, Jane. This is almost the last meal you will eat at Thornfield Hall for a long time.'

I sat down near him, but told him I could not eat.

'Is it because you are worried about the journey, Jane? What a bright spot of colour you have on each cheek! And how strangely your eyes are shining! Are you well?'

'I believe I am. I wish that the present hour would never end.

Who knows what will happen in the next?'

'You are too excited, Jane, and you are tired. Give me your confidence: tell me what is troubling you.'

'Then, sir, listen. Last night, for some time after I went to bed, I could not sleep. A storm was rising, but beneath the noise it made I seemed to hear another sound, like the wild cry of some dog in the distance. When I slept at last, it was to dream that Thornfield Hall was a ruin.'

'Is that all, Jane?'

'All the introduction, sir; the story is still to come. When I woke, a beam of light was shining in my eyes. I thought it was daylight, but I was mistaken. It was only candlelight. The servant, I supposed, had come in. There was a light on the table, and the door of the cupboard where, before going to bed, I had hung my wedding dress and veil, stood open. I heard a movement there. I asked, "What are you doing?" No one answered, but a figure came out of the cupboard. It took the light, held it up, and examined the clothes there. I called out again, and still it was silent. I had risen from my bed, and I bent forward. I was filled with surprise, and then my blood ran cold. Mr Rochester, this was not a servant, it was not Mrs Fairfax, it was not – no, I am sure of it – it was not even that strange woman, Grace Poole.'

'It must have been one of them,' interrupted my master.

'No, sir.'

'Describe it, Jane.'

'It seemed, sir, to be a woman, tall, with thick dark hair hanging down her back. In a little while she picked up my veil and threw it over her own head. She looked in the mirror, and I saw her features shown in it. They were a fearful sight – unnatural, wild and rough. Then, sir, she removed the veil, tore it in two and, throwing the pieces on the floor, crushed them with her foot.'

'And afterwards?'

'The figure moved back to the door. Just at my bedside it stopped, held the candle close to my face, and put the flame out under my eyes. I was conscious of her face flaming over mine, and then I fainted; for the second time in my life, I lost my senses from terror.'

'Who was with you when you woke?'

'No one. It was day. I rose and bathed my head and face in water. Though weak, I was not ill. I have kept this secret. Now, sir, tell me who and what that woman was.'

'The invention of your excited brain, that is certain.'

'I wish I could believe you, sir. But when I got up and looked round the room, there, on the rug, I saw the veil, torn from top to bottom in two halves!'

Mr Rochester made a movement of surprise.

'Thank God it was only the veil that was harmed! Now, Jane, I'll explain it to you. It was half-dream, half-reality. I have no doubt that a woman did enter your room. It must have been Grace Poole. In a state between waking and sleeping, you got a false idea of her appearance. The tearing of the veil was real, and it is the sort of thing she does. You will ask why I keep such a woman in my house, and when we have been married a year, I will tell you. Are you satisfied?'

I considered. It appeared to be the only possible solution. I was not satisfied, but I tried to appear so, to please him.

'You must sleep in Adèle's room tonight,' said Mr Rochester. 'I would prefer that you did not sleep alone. Lock the door on the inside. And now, Jane, no more fearful thoughts.'

I never slept at all. As soon as the sun rose, I rose too.

Chapter 29   The Wedding

A servant came at seven the next morning to dress me. She took a long time, and when I went down Mr Rochester was waiting impatiently at the foot of the stairs. He told me he would give me only ten minutes to eat some breakfast. At the same time he ordered the luggage and the carriage to be brought to the door.

'Jane, are you ready?'

I rose. There were no guests, no relations to wait for. Mr Rochester hurried me out of the house.

I can still remember the old grey church outside the gates of Thornfield, rising calmly in front of me with the red morning sky beyond. I have not forgotten, either, the figures of two strangers wandering about the churchyard, who passed round to the back of the church when they saw us. They were not noticed by Mr Rochester, who was looking into my face with great seriousness.

We entered the quiet building and took our places. The priest and the clerk were waiting. All was still. The only movement was that of two shadows in a far corner. The service began.

The clergyman explained the purpose and duties of marriage, and then came a step forward, and, bending slightly towards Mr Rochester, went on:

'I must now ask you both, if either of you know of any reason why you may not be lawfully joined together in marriage, to admit it now.'

He paused, according to custom. When is the pause after that sentence ever broken by reply? Not, perhaps, once in a hundred years. The clergyman had not even lifted his eyes from his book; he had waited a moment, and was continuing, when a voice said:

'The marriage cannot take place. I know of something which prevents it.'

The priest looked at the speaker. It was one of the strangers whom I had noticed earlier. Mr Rochester turned slightly towards him. He took my hand.

'The ceremony must be broken off,' repeated the voice. 'I am in a position to prove my claim that it would be unlawful.'

The clergyman looked uncertain.

'What is the nature of the difficulty? Perhaps it may be explained away?'

'Hardly,' was the answer. Pronouncing each word plainly, calmly, steadily, the speaker continued:

'It simply consists in the existence of a previous marriage. Mr Rochester has a wife now living.'

I looked at Mr Rochester: I made him look at me. His whole face was like colourless rock; his eyes, though, flamed and flashed. Without speaking, without smiling, he simply put his arm around my waist and held me to his side.

'Who are you?' he asked the stranger.

'My name is Briggs. I am a lawyer.'

'And you claim that I have a wife?'

'I am reminding you of the lady's existence, sir, which the law recognizes, if you do not.'

'Give me an account of her – her name, her family.'

'Certainly.'

Mr Briggs took a paper from his pocket and read in a calm voice:

'I state and can prove that Edward Rochester, of Thornfield Hall, was married to my sister, Bertha Mason, at Spanish Town, Jamaica, 15 years ago. The details of the marriage will be found in the church records there. A copy is now in my possession. Signed, Richard Mason.'

'If that is a true statement, it may prove that I have been married, but it does not prove that the woman mentioned in it is still living.'

'She was living three months ago. I have a witness to the fact.'

'Where is he?'

'He is present. Mr Mason, have the goodness to step forward.'

Mr Rochester, on hearing the name, shook uncontrollably. I felt a sudden movement of anger or despair run through him. The second stranger, who had until now remained in the shadows, came closer. A pale face looked over the lawyer's shoulder. It was Mason himself. Mr Rochester turned and fixed him with his eyes. He moved towards him and lifted his strong arm – he could have struck Mason, knocked him to the church floor, but the man stepped back trembling, and cried out faintly.

'Sir,' said the priest, 'do not forget where you are.' Then, addressing Mason, he inquired gently, 'Do you know, sir, whether this gentleman's wife is still living?'

'She is now living at Thornfield Hall,' said Mason, in a low, uncertain voice. 'I saw her there last April.'

'At Thornfield Hall!' cried the clergyman. 'Impossible! I have lived for many years in this neighbourhood, sir, and never heard of a Mrs Rochester there.'

I saw a bitter smile twist Mr Rochester's lips, and he said between his teeth:

'No, by God! I took care that none should hear of her under that name.' He was silent for some minutes, and then went on, 'Enough! Everything shall be made known immediately. Close your book. There will be no wedding today.'

And Mr Rochester began his story:

Chapter 30   Mr Rochester's Story

'I am little better than a devil at this moment, and deserve no doubt the severest judgments of God. Gentlemen, my plan is destroyed. What this lawyer and his witness say is true. The clergyman here says he has never heard of a Mrs Rochester at the

Hall, but I suppose he has listened at some time or other to talk about the mysterious madwoman kept there under lock and key. I can now inform you that she is my wife, sister of this brave-hearted person here, with his white face and trembling body. Bertha Mason is mad, and she came from a mad family, weak-minded and violent. Her mother was both a madwoman and a heavy drinker – as I found out after I had married the daughter, because they were silent on family secrets before then. Bertha copied her parent in both ways.

'My father was to blame for the situation I now find myself in. I was not the oldest son. I had a brother once, older than I. My father was not a generous man, and could not bear the idea of dividing his property so as to leave me a fair share. Everything, he decided, should go to my brother. But he could not bear that a son of his should be a poor man. I must be provided for by a wealthy marriage. Mr Mason, from the West Indies, had been known to him for a long time. He had a son and a daughter, and my father learnt that he would give the daughter a fortune of thirty thousand pounds. That was enough for my father. When I left college, I was sent out to Jamaica to marry a bride already chosen for me. My father said nothing about her money, but he told me that Miss Mason was the pride of Spanish Town for her beauty, and this was no lie. I found her a fine woman, in the style of Blanche Ingram. They showed her to me at parties, beautifully dressed. I rarely saw her alone, and had very little private conversation with her. All the men seemed to admire her and be jealous of me. I was attracted and, being young and inexperienced, I thought that I loved her. Her relations encouraged me; competitors made me jealous; and a marriage was performed almost before I knew it.

'Later, the truth was made known to me. My wife's beauty disappeared, and her weaknesses developed until they were as bad as they could be. My brother had died, and at the end of four years my father died too. I was rich now, but in happiness poorer than a slave.

'I brought my wife to England, and had a terrible journey with such a creature on the ship. I hired Grace Poole, who had worked in a madhouse, to keep watch over her. She and Carter, the doctor, are the only two who have ever learnt my secret. Mrs Fairfax may have suspected something, but she could have had no exact knowledge of the facts. Grace has, on the whole, shown herself to be a good keeper, though owing to an occasional tendency to drink, she has once or twice allowed my wife to escape.

'But I owe you no further explanation. Gentlemen, I invite you to come up to the house and visit Mrs Poole's patient, and *my wife!* This girl,' he continued, looking at me, 'knew nothing of the disgusting secret. She thought that all was fair and lawful. Come, all of you – follow!'

Still holding me tightly, he left the church. The three gentlemen followed. At the front door of the Hall we found the carriage.

'Take it back to the coachhouse,' said Mr Rochester. 'It will not be needed today.'

As we entered, Mrs Fairfax, Adèle, and the servants came forward to greet us.

'Away with your good wishes!' cried the master. 'Who wants them? Not I! They are 15 years too late.'

He passed on and went up the stairs to the top floor. The low, black door, opened by his key, admitted us to the room where Mason had lain wounded. He opened the inner door and we entered.

In a room without a window burnt a fire guarded by high, strong bars. A lamp hung from the roof by a chain. Grace Poole bent over the fire cooking something in a pot. In the deep shade, at the furthest end of the room, a figure ran backwards and forwards. What it was, whether animal or human being, one could not at first sight tell. It seemed to run across the floor on four legs; it made strange animal-like noises; but it was covered with clothing, and a quantity of dark, greyish hair hid its face and head.

'Good morning, Mrs Poole,' said Mr Rochester. 'How is she today?'

'Fair, sir,' replied Grace, lifting the boiling pot carefully off the fire.

An angry cry suggested that this report was mistaken. The clothed animal rose, and stood upright.

'Ah, sir, she has seen you!' cried Grace. 'You'd better not stay. Take care!'

The madwoman screamed. She pushed her disordered hair back from her face and looked wildly at her visitors. I recognized those ugly features. Mrs Poole walked towards her.

'Keep out of the way,' said Mr Rochester. 'She has no knife now, I suppose, and I'm on my guard.'

'Take care!' cried Grace.

The three gentlemen moved back quickly. Mr Rochester pushed me behind him. The madwoman jumped at him, seized his throat and bit into his cheek. They struggled. She was a big woman, almost as tall as her husband, and strong as well. He could have settled her with a well-directed blow, but he did not hit her. At last he seized her arms and tied her to a chair with some rope which was at hand. The operation was performed with the wildest screams from the madwoman. Mr Rochester then turned to the men who were watching, with a smile both bitter and despairing.

'That is *my wife*,' he said, 'and *this* is what I wished to have,' he added, laying his hands on my shoulder, 'this young girl who stands so calmly and quietly. Look at the difference, then judge me if you can.'

We all left the room except Mr Rochester, who stayed behind for a moment to give some further order to Grace Poole. The lawyer addressed me as he went downstairs.

'You, madam,' he said, 'are cleared from all blame. Your uncle will be glad to hear it – if, in fact, he is still alive.'

'My uncle! Do you know him?'

'Mr Mason does. Mr Eyre has been the Madeira representative of his business for some years. When your uncle received your letter mentioning the coming marriage between yourself and Mr Rochester, Mr Mason happened to be with him. Mr Eyre told him the news, as he had learnt that Mr Mason knew a Mr Rochester. Mr Mason, shocked and troubled, told him the real state of affairs. Your uncle, who, I am sorry to say, is now very ill, and not likely to live, could not hurry to England himself to save you from the trap into which you had fallen, but he begged Mr Mason to return here immediately to try to prevent the false marriage, and he asked me to help Mr Mason. If I were not certain that your uncle will be dead before you could reach Madeira, I would advise you to go there with Mr Mason. As it is, I think you had better remain in England until you hear further, either from Mr Eyre himself or from me. Have we anything else to stay for?' he inquired of Mr Mason.

'No, no – let us be gone,' was the anxious reply, and without waiting to speak to Mr Rochester, they went out of the hall door. The clergyman followed soon afterwards.

I heard him go as I stood at the half-open door of my room, to which I had now returned. I shut myself in, locked the door, and began – not to cry, because I was still too calm for that – to take off the wedding dress and replace it with the simple dress that I had worn the day before, as I thought, for the last time. I then sat down. I felt weak and tired. I leaned my arms on a table, and my head dropped on them. Until now, I had only heard, seen, moved, and watched one event follow another. Now I began to think.

Jane Eyre, who had been an eager, happy woman – almost a bride – was a cold, lonely girl again. Her hopes were all dead. That bitter hour cannot be described: I came, in truth, into deep waters, and the floods covered me.

Chapter 31   Flight

Some time in the afternoon I raised my head and, looking round, asked myself: 'What shall I do?'

The answer my mind gave: 'Leave Thornfield immediately,' came so quickly, and was so terrible, that I closed my ears to it. I could not do it. But then a voice within me repeated that I could and must. I struggled with my own willpower. Necessity and passion fought until, tired out with mental suffering and weak with hunger, I fell asleep.

It was soon after midnight that I rose and, taking nothing except my money and a few things, softly left my room. I would have gone past Mr Rochester's room without a pause, but my heart stopped its beat for a moment at his door, and my foot was forced to stop too. I heard him walking around restlessly inside. He would send for me in the morning. I would be gone. He would suffer, perhaps sink into despair. I thought about this, and then moved on.

From the kitchen I took some water and some bread. Without a sound I opened the door and went outside.

A mile away, beyond the fields, lay a road which stretched in the opposite direction to Millcote, a road that I had never travelled along but often noticed. Towards this I directed my steps.

I walked on and on. The short summer night was nearly over, and birds began to sing in the trees. Birds were loyal to their loves. And I? I hated myself. Still, I could not turn back. God must have led me on. I was crying wildly as I walked along, fast, fast, like one out of her mind. Finally I felt faint and weak, and I fell.

I lay on the ground for some minutes. I had some fear – or hope – that I might die, but I was soon up again, as determined as ever to reach the road.

When I got there I heard wheels, and saw a coach coming along. I stopped it and asked to be taken as far as the pound I had would pay for. The inside was empty. I entered, and the coach rolled on its way.

Chapter 32   Despair

It was evening the following day when the coach left me at a place where four roads met. It drove on, and I was soon alone. It was then I discovered that I had forgotten to take my things out of the coach. I had nothing left in the world.

The signpost told me that the nearest town was ten miles away. There were great hills behind and on each side of me. There were chains of mountains far beyond the deep valley at my feet. I saw no travellers on the road.

What could I do? Where should I go? I touched the grass; it was dry, and still warm with the heat of the sun. The sky was clear, and there was no wind. Tonight I would be Nature's guest: she would give me food and shelter without charge. I had one piece of bread left. I picked a handful of wild berries and ate them with the bread. I had some rest that night, but it was broken by a sad heart.

The next day I followed a road which led away from the hot sun. I was weak and tired when at last I heard a bell – a church bell. Human life and human activity were near. A little later I entered a village. At the bottom of its one street there was a little shop with some bread in the window.

I went into the shop. A woman was there. Seeing a respectably dressed person, probably a lady, she came forward politely. How could she serve me? I was seized with shame, because I had no money. My tongue would not pronounce the request for food that I had intended to make. I only begged permission to sit down for a minute. Disappointed, she coldly pointed to a chair.

After a little while, I asked if there was a dressmaker in the village.

'Yes, two or three. Quite as many as there is employment for.'

'Do you know of any place in the neighbourhood where a servant is wanted?'

'No, I do not.'

I went on a little longer, but she seemed tired of my questions. In the end I took off my hat, and asked if she would give me a loaf of bread for it.

She looked at me with suspicion.

'No, I never sell food in that way. How can I tell where you got it?'

An ordinary beggar is often an object of distrust; a well-dressed one is always so. I could not blame the woman. I left the village in despair. The rest of the day I begged, but without success.

I spent the night in a wood. It was not dry, and towards morning it rained. Another day went by, as hopeless as the first. I began to wish for death.

Towards evening on the next day I saw a faint light in the distance and dragged my tired body slowly in its direction. A white gate could just be seen in the growing darkness. I passed through it and came to a kitchen window. A candle was burning on a table, and an oldish woman, rather rough-looking but very clean, was sewing by its light.

A group of greater interest appeared near the fireside. Two

115

young, graceful women – ladies in every way – sat, one in an armchair, and the other on a lower seat. Both were dressed in black. A large old dog rested its head on the knee of one girl, and the other girl was stroking a black cat.

This poor kitchen was a strange place for such people! Who were they? I had nowhere seen such faces as theirs, but, as I looked at them, I seemed to be familiar with every feature. They were pale and thoughtful-looking, and each bent over a book, while two other great books, which they frequently turned to, lay on the floor beside them: perhaps dictionaries to help them in the work of translation.

I watched them for a long time. At last the oldish woman began to prepare a meal. I went to the door and knocked. She opened it.

'What do you want?' she inquired, in a voice of surprise.

'May I speak to the young ladies?'

'You had better tell me what you have to say to them. Where do you come from?'

'I am a stranger.'

'What is your business here at this hour?'

'I want a night's shelter in some corner, and a bit of bread.'

Distrust, the feeling that I feared most, appeared in the woman's face. 'I'll give you a piece of bread,' she said, after a pause, 'but we can't take a wanderer in to sleep.'

'Where shall I go if you drive me away?'

'Oh, I'm sure you know where to go and what to do. Here is a coin. Move away now.'

The honest but unsympathetic servant shut the door and locked it from the inside.

This was the end. Weak as I was, I could not go another step. I sank down outside the door and cried.

'I can only die,' I said out loud. 'Let me wait for God's will in silence.'

'All men must die,' said a voice quite near me, 'but not all are meant to do so in their youth.'

'Who is speaking?' I asked, frightened at the unexpected sound.

The newcomer knocked loudly on the door.

'Is that you, Mr St John?' cried the servant.

'Yes, yes. Open quickly, Hannah.'

'Well, how wet and cold you must be on a night like this! Come in. Your sisters have been quite anxious about you. There has been a beggar-woman. I believe she has not gone yet. Get up, for shame! Move off, I say!'

'Be silent, Hannah. You have done your duty; now let me do mine. I think this is a special case.' And, turning to me, he told me to go before him into the house.

I obeyed him with difficulty. Soon I was in that clean, bright kitchen, with the whole family looking at me. My head seemed to spin: I fell, but a chair received me. One of the sisters broke some bread, dipped it in milk, and put it to my lips. There was pity in her face. I tasted what was offered me – weakly at first, then more eagerly.

'No more at present, Diana. She has no strength; it will harm her. See if she can speak now. Ask her her name.'

I answered: 'My name is Jane Elliott.' I was anxious that my true name should not be discovered.

'Where do you live? Where are your friends?'

I was silent.

'Can you send for anyone you know?'

I shook my head.

Somehow, once I had entered this house and been brought face to face with its owners, I no longer felt like a wanderer who belonged nowhere. I no longer felt like a beggar, and my natural manner began to come back to me. When Mr St John demanded an account of myself, I said after a short pause:

'Sir, I can give you no details tonight.'

'What, then, do you expect me to do for you?'

'Nothing.' I had only enough strength for short answers.

Diana now spoke. 'Do you mean that you have now received the help that you need, and that we may send you back out into the rainy night?'

I looked at her. She had, I thought, an unusual face, expressive of both power and goodness. I took sudden courage. Answering her sympathetic look with a smile, I said:

'I will trust you. If I were a masterless and homeless dog, I know you would not turn me away tonight. As it is, I have no fear. Do as you like with me, but excuse me from much speech – it hurts me to use my voice.'

All three looked at me in silence.

'Hannah,' said Mr St John at last, 'let her sit here for now, and ask her no more questions. In ten minutes more, give her the rest of the bread and milk. Mary and Diana, let us go into the sitting room and discuss the matter.'

They went out. Very soon one of the ladies returned and gave some directions to Hannah. Before long I was helped upstairs into a warm, dry bed. I thanked God and, with a warm feeling of grateful joy, I fell asleep.

Chapter 33   The Rivers Family

The memory of the three days and nights following this is very faint in my mind. I knew I was in a small room and in a narrow bed. I noticed when anyone entered or left; I could understand what was said when someone was near me; but to open my lips or move any part of my body was impossible.

Hannah, the servant, was my most frequent visitor. I felt that she was unsure of me. Diana and Mary appeared once or twice a day. They whispered at my bedside, wondering who I might be, and thankful that they had not failed to give me shelter. Never once in their conversation did I hear a word of doubt about the kindness they had shown me, or of suspicion or dislike of myself. I was comforted.

Mr St John came only once. He looked at me and said that my state of weakness was the result of extreme and continued tiredness. He said it was unnecessary to send for a doctor:

'Nature will manage best if left to herself. There is no illness.' These opinions he stated in a few words, in a quiet, low voice. He stood watching me for some minutes, then added: 'She seems sensible, but is not at all good-looking.'

On the third day I was better; on the fourth I could speak, move, sit up in bed, and turn. I began to feel hungry, and when in the afternoon I found on a chair near me all my own clothes, cleaned of the mud of my wanderings, I succeeded with some difficulty in dressing myself. Feeling respectable again, I climbed slowly down a stone staircase.

I found Hannah baking in the kitchen. When she saw that I was tidy and well dressed, she looked more approving. She even smiled.

'Well, you have got up!' she said. 'You are better, then. You may sit in my chair by the fire, if you wish.'

She moved around busily, examining me occasionally out of the corner of her eye. Turning to me as she took some bread from the fire, she asked:

'Did you ever go begging before you came here?'

I was annoyed for a moment; then remembering how I had first appeared to her, I answered quietly but firmly:

'You are mistaken in thinking that I am a beggar. I am no more so than yourself or your young ladies.'

After a pause she said:

'I don't understand. You have no house or money, I imagine?'

'The lack of house or money does not make me a beggar in your meaning of the word.'

'Are you educated?' she asked, a little later.

'Yes.'

She opened her eyes wide.

'Then why cannot you support yourself?'

'I have supported myself, and I hope I shall do so again. And now, never mind what I have been, but tell me the name of the family whom you serve.'

'Their name is Rivers.'

'Does the gentleman live here?'

'No, he is only staying for a little while. He is a clergyman, and works at Morton, a few miles away.'

'Their father is dead?'

'Yes, he died three weeks ago.'

'They have no mother?'

'She has been dead many years. I have been here for 30 years, and looked after all three.'

'That proves that you have been honest and loyal. I say that to praise you, though you had the rudeness to call me a beggar, and refused me help when I was in trouble.'

She gave me a look of surprise.

'I believe I was mistaken,' she said. 'You must not think too badly of me.'

I continued rather severely:

'But I do think badly of you – not so much because you refused me shelter, but because you blamed me for having no possessions. You should not consider it a crime to be poor.'

'That is true,' she admitted. 'Mr St John told me so, too. I see that I was wrong.'

'Enough. I forgive you. Shake hands.'

She put out her rough hand and smiled. From that moment we were friends.

Hannah was a great talker, and as she worked, she told me the history of the Rivers family. Their father had been a gentleman of good family who had lost a great deal of money by trusting a man who gave him bad advice. As he was not rich enough to give his daughters fortunes, they had taken positions as governesses. They were only now at home for a few weeks on account of their father's death. To be united and in their own house was their greatest happiness.

Soon the two ladies, who had been out for a walk to Morton, returned with their brother. Mr St John, when he saw me, only smiled as he walked through the kitchen, but his sisters stopped. Mary quietly expressed the pleasure she felt in seeing me able to come down. Diana took my hand and shook her head at me.

'You should have waited for my permission to come down,' she said. 'You still look very pale. And why are you in here? Mary and I sit in the kitchen sometimes, because at home we like to be free, but you are a guest and must go into the sitting room.'

Still holding my hand, she made me rise and led me into the inner room. She closed the door, leaving me alone with Mr St John, who sat opposite me reading. I examined him and the room.

The sitting room was rather small, and everything in it looked both well worn and well cared for. Mr St John, still as stone, was young – perhaps twenty-eight to thirty – with pure, straight features. His eyes were blue, his forehead high and colourless, his hair fair. He gave one a feeling, not of gentleness, but of hidden force. He did not speak one word to me until his sisters returned, bringing tea.

I ate eagerly. Mr Rivers now closed his book and directed his eyes at me.

'You are very hungry,' he said.

'I trust I shall not eat your food for long, sir,' was my awkward reply.

'No,' he said carefully. 'When you have told us the address of your friends, we can write to them and you can go back to them.'

'That, I must tell you plainly, is impossible.'

The three looked at me, not with distrust, but with interest. I speak particularly of the ladies. St John's eyes seemed to be less able to express his own thoughts than to search out those of others.

'Do you mean to say that you are completely without family?'

'I have no tie to any living person in the whole of England.'

He looked quickly at my hands before he spoke. 'You have never been married?'

As I replied to this, I felt my face burn. They all saw my confusion. Diana and Mary helped me by turning their eyes elsewhere, but their colder and severer brother continued to fix his eyes on me.

'Where did you last live?' he now asked.

'You are asking too many questions, St John,' murmured Mary in a low voice.

'That is my secret,' I replied shortly.

'Which, in my opinion, you have a right to keep from everybody if you wish,' remarked Diana.

'If I know nothing of you and your history, I cannot help you,' he said. 'And you need help, don't you?'

'I need help from some good person in finding work that I can do and that will allow me to support myself.'

'Tell me, then, what you *can* do.'

'Mr Rivers,' I said, turning to him and looking at him openly, 'you and your sisters have done me a great service. You have a certain claim, not only to my thanks, but also to my trust. I will tell you as much about myself as I can without harming my peace of mind and the private affairs of myself and others.

'I am an orphan, educated at Lowood School. I left it nearly a year ago to become a governess. I was forced to leave my post for a reason that I cannot explain. I was not in any way to blame. I thought only of speed and secrecy in getting away, and in my troubled state of mind I failed to take out of the coach by which I travelled the small amount of my possessions that I was able to bring away with me. In this position I found myself helpless and with failing strength until you, Mr Rivers, took me under the shelter of your roof.'

'Don't make her talk any more, St John,' said Diana, as I paused. 'She is clearly not yet fit for excitement. Come to the fire and sit down now, Miss Elliott.'

I made a sudden movement of surprise; I had forgotten my new name. Mr Rivers, whom nothing seemed to escape, noticed it immediately.

'You said your name is Jane Elliott?' he remarked.

'I did say so, and it is the name by which I think it wise to be called at present.'

'You would not like to be our guest for very long?'

'All I ask is that you will show me some means of getting work. Until then, allow me to stay here. I am afraid of being homeless again.'

'You *shall* of course stay here,' said Diana.

'You *shall*,' repeated Mary.

'My sisters, you see, are happy to have you as their guest,' said Mr St John. 'I prefer to put you in a position to support yourself, and I shall try to do so, but I work in a poor area, so my help will not be great.'

I repeated that I would be pleased to accept any means of employment that he might offer me, and soon after went back upstairs, since I had nearly come to the end of my strength again.

Chapter 34   Hopes and Disappointments

The more I came to know Diana and Mary, the better I liked them. In a few days I felt well enough to sit up all day and walk out sometimes. I could join the sisters in everything they did, and in doing this I now enjoyed for the first time the pleasure that comes from perfect agreement in taste, feelings and ideas.

They loved their home and the wild country around it, and I too soon learned to feel the attraction of the place. Indoors we were equally happy companions. I liked to read the books they lent me. They were both more skilled than I, but I followed with eagerness the path of knowledge that they had travelled before me. Diana offered to teach me German, and I in turn gave lessons in drawing to Mary. In this way, days passed like hours, and weeks like days.

As to Mr St John, the close friendship which had formed between me and his sisters did not include him. One reason was that he was rarely at home. He spent a great deal of his time visiting the sick and poor in his neighbourhood. No bad weather seemed to keep him from these clergyman's duties.

But besides his frequent absences, there was another difficulty in building a friendship with him. He seemed to have a lonely nature, living a life apart from others. The first real sign of his character came when I heard him speak in his own church. He spoke with calmness that grew into force. My heart was moved, my mind surprised by the power of his words, but neither was softened.

A month passed. Diana and Mary would soon return to their posts in the south of England, and St John had said nothing to me about my future, a problem that was now becoming urgent.

One morning, finding myself alone with him for a few minutes, I was brave enough to move towards the corner of the sitting room which was kept specially for his use. I did not know how to begin, but he saved me the trouble.

Looking up as I came near, he said:

'You have a question to ask me?'

'Yes. I wish to know whether you have heard of any employment for me.'

'I found something for you three weeks ago, but as you seemed both happy and useful here, and your society gave my sisters unusual pleasure, I judged it unnecessary to break in on your comfort until they left.'

'What is the work you have found for me?'

'It is nothing very profitable, but I consider that nothing that can improve our race is too unimportant an activity. I believe you will accept it for a time, though I do not think it will satisfy your nature for ever.'

'Do explain,' I urged.

'I will. I shall not stay long at Morton now that my father is dead, but while I am here I shall do my best to improve it. I have already started a school for poor boys, and I intend now to open a second one for girls. I have hired a building, with a small house for the school teacher. Her salary will be thirty pounds a year. A rich lady in the neighbourhood is providing financial support. Will you be the school teacher?'

'I thank you for the offer, Mr Rivers, and I accept it with all my heart.'

'But you understand me? It is a village school. Your pupils will be only poor girls – the daughters of farm workers. Sewing, reading, writing, simple sums, will be all that you will have to teach. What will you do with your skills?'

'Save them until they are wanted. They will keep.'

He smiled now, well pleased.

Diana and Mary became sadder and more silent as the day came closer when they had to leave their brother and their home. As if to prove the truth of the old saying that "misfortunes never come one at a time", news came to add to their disappointments. St John entered one day with a letter.

'Your Uncle John is dead,' he said. 'Read this.'

Both sisters did so in silence. They all smiled rather sadly.

'After all, we are no poorer than we were before,' remarked Mary.

Diana turned to me.

'Jane, you will be surprised at us and our mysteries,' she said, 'and think us hard-hearted for not feeling more at the death of so near a relation, but we have never seen or known him. He was our mother's brother. My father and he quarrelled because it was through his advice that my father lost all his money. They parted in anger and were never friends afterwards. My uncle became rich, but did not marry. My father always hoped that he would put right the wrong he had done by leaving us his possessions when he died. This letter informs us that he has left everything to his only other relation. He had a right, of course, to do as he pleased, but we cannot help feeling for the moment a little disappointed. Even a small amount of money would have made a great deal of difference to us.'

After this explanation, the subject was not mentioned any more. The next day I left to begin my new life, and the sisters set out for the south.

Chapter 35   New Experiences

I carried on the work of the village school as actively as I could. It was truly hard at first, and some time passed before I could understand my pupils and their characters. Completely untaught, they seemed at first sight hopelessly dull, but I soon found that I was mistaken. Many of them had excellent intelligence and began to take pleasure in doing their work well. The speed of their progress was sometimes surprising, and I felt an honest and happy pride in it. Their parents were grateful and showed me respect. In time I felt I was becoming popular in the area.

But after a day spent in honourable work among my pupils, and an evening passed in drawing or reading happily alone, I used to rush into strange dreams at night – stormy dreams, where, among unusual scenes, full of adventure, I met Mr Rochester again and again, always at some exciting moment, and the hope of passing my life by his side returned with all its first force and fire. Then I awoke, and in the still, dark night I gave way to despair.

One day was a holiday. It was the afternoon and I had tidied the house and was doing some drawing when, after one rapid knock, my door opened and St John Rivers came in.

'I have come to see how you are spending your free time,' he said. 'Not, I hope, in thought? No, that is good. While you draw, you will not feel lonely. I have brought you a book for the evening.'

As I was eagerly looking through the pages, St John bent to examine my drawing. When he had finished, he pulled over it the sheet of thin paper on which I used to rest my hand, to prevent me rubbing the surface of the drawing. What he suddenly saw on this empty piece of paper it was impossible for me to tell, but something had attracted his attention. He picked the paper up and gave me a look which was inexpressibly strange and quite beyond my understanding. His lips opened as if to speak; but he kept back the coming sentence, whatever it was.

'What is the matter?'

'Nothing in the world,' was the reply, and, as he replaced the paper, I saw him neatly tear off a narrow piece from the edge. It disappeared into his pocket, and, with a quick 'good afternoon', he went away.

I, in my turn, examined the paper, but saw nothing on it

except a few dull spots of paint. I puzzled over the mystery for a minute or two, but, finding no explanation, I soon dismissed it from my mind.

Chapter 36 The Heiress

When St John left, it was beginning to snow, and the storm continued all night. The next day an icy wind brought fresh falls, and by evening it was almost impossible to move out of doors. My surprise, therefore, was very great when the door suddenly opened and St John Rivers appeared, his tall figure almost completely covered with snow.

'Is there any bad news?' I asked. 'Has anything happened?'

'No. How very easily you become anxious!' he answered, removing his coat and shaking the snow from his boots. 'I am spoiling your clean floor, but you must excuse me for once.'

'But why have you come?'

'Rather an unwelcoming question to put to a visitor. I only wished to have a talk with you. Since yesterday I have been experiencing the excitement of a person to whom a story has been half told, and who is impatient to hear its ending.'

He sat down, and I waited, but he seemed lost in his own thoughts. I went on with the reading which his entrance had interrupted. In a little while he took a letter from his pocket, looked at it in silence, and at last spoke.

'Leave your book a moment, and come a little nearer to the fire.'

Wondering, I obeyed.

'A little while ago,' he went on, 'I spoke of a half-finished story. I am going to repeat it to you. It is only fair to warn you that some of it will sound familiar.

'Twenty years ago, a poor clergyman – never mind his name –

loved a rich man's daughter. She returned his love, and married him against the advice of all her friends. Before two years had passed, both were dead. They left a daughter, a friendless thing, brought up by an aunt called Mrs Reed, of Gateshead. What is it? Did you hear a noise? The orphan passed at the age of ten to a place you know – Lowood – where she left an honourable record as a pupil and a teacher. She became a governess at the house of a certain Mr Rochester.'

'Mr Rivers!' I interrupted.

'I have nearly finished. I know nothing of Mr Rochester, except that he pretended to offer honourable marriage to this young girl, and that at the last moment she found out that he had a wife still alive, though a madwoman. Soon after that, an event happened which made inquiry after the governess necessary. It was then discovered that she had gone – no one could tell when, where, or how. But it has become a matter of urgency that she should be found. Advertisements have been put in all the newspapers. I myself received a letter from a certain Mr Briggs, a lawyer, giving me these details.'

'But tell me,' I said. 'What about Mr Rochester? Is he well?'

'I have no knowledge of anything concerning Mr Rochester, except for his attempt to deceive the law.'

'But these people wrote to him?'

'Mr Briggs states that the answer to his request for information was signed by a lady: Alice Fairfax. This Mr Rochester must have been a bad man,' remarked Mr Rivers.

'You don't know him. Don't give an opinion on him,' I said.

St John took from his pocket a piece of paper marked with spots of paint. I read on it, in my own handwriting, the words "Jane Eyre", no doubt written in some careless moment.

'Briggs wrote to me of a Jane Eyre,' he said, 'and the advertisements demanded someone of that name. I knew a Jane Elliott, and I had my suspicions. This piece of paper told me the truth yesterday. You admit to your real name?'

'Yes, but where is Mr Briggs? Perhaps he knows more about Mr Rochester than you do.'

'Mr Briggs is in London, but I doubt whether he is interested in Mr Rochester. You have not asked why he is interested in you – why he is searching for you?'

'Well, what did he want?'

'Only to tell you that your uncle, Mr Eyre of Madeira, is dead, that he has left you all his property, and that you are now rich – only that – nothing more.'

'I! Rich?'

'Yes, quite an heiress.'

There was silence.

Chapter 37   Relations

It is a fine thing to be lifted in a moment to wealth, but not something that one can really enjoy immediately. Besides, my uncle, my only relation, whom I had hoped one day to see, was dead.

'You are raising your forehead at last,' said Mr Rivers. 'Perhaps you will now ask how much you are worth?'

'How much am I worth?'

'Oh, just a little! Nothing to speak of – twenty thousand pounds.'

'Twenty thousand pounds!'

'Well,' said St John, laughing, a thing I had never known him to do before, 'if you were guilty of a murder, and I told you that your crime was discovered, you could hardly look more worried.'

'It is a large amount. Don't you think there is a mistake?'

'No mistake at all.'

Mr Rivers now rose and said good night. His hand was on the door, when a sudden thought came to me.

'Stop one minute!' I cried.

'Well?'

'It puzzles me to know why Mr Briggs wrote to you about me, or how he knew you or could imagine that you, living in such a lonely place as this, had the power to help in discovering me.'

'Oh, I am a clergyman, and clergymen are often asked for help about various matters.'

'No. That does not satisfy me!' I cried. 'I must know more about this business.'

'Another time.'

'No! Tonight!' and as he turned from the door, I placed myself between it and him. He looked rather embarrassed.

'I would rather Diana or Mary informed you.'

My eagerness only increased, and I demanded once more to be satisfied.

'But I warn you I am a hard man,' he said, 'difficult to persuade.'

'And I am a hard woman – impossible to refuse.'

'Well,' he said, 'I give way, if not to your eagerness, to your determination. Besides, you must know some day – it may as well be now as later. Your name is Jane Eyre?'

'Of course – that was settled before.'

'You do not know, perhaps, that I am called St John Eyre Rivers?'

'No, I do not! I remember now seeing the letter E in your name written in books you have lent me. But what then? Surely . . .'

I stopped. The truth came to me as details began to connect themselves in my mind. St John went on:

'My mother's name was Eyre. She had two brothers, one a priest who married Miss Jane Reed of Gateshead, the other John Eyre of Madeira. Mr Briggs, being Mr Eyre's lawyer, wrote to us last August to inform us of our uncle's death, and to say that he had left his property to the orphan daughter of his brother the clergyman. He had left nothing to us as a result of a quarrel, never forgiven, between him and my father. Mr Briggs wrote again, a few weeks later, to say that the heiress was lost, and asking if we knew anything of her. A name written on a piece of paper has allowed me to find her. You know the rest.'

'Do let me speak,' I said. 'Your mother was my father's sister?'

'Yes.'

'My Uncle John was your Uncle John? You, Diana and Mary are my cousins?'

'We are cousins, yes.'

I looked at him. This was true wealth, wealth to the heart.

'Oh, I am glad!' I cried.

St John smiled.

'Did I not say you ignored important points for much less important matters?' he asked. 'You were serious when I told you that you now have a fortune, and you are excited because you have cousins.'

'What can you mean? It may be of no importance to you. You have sisters, and don't care about a cousin. But I had nobody, and now I have three relations. I say again, I am glad!'

I walked quickly up and down. Thoughts rose more rapidly than I could express them. Mr Rivers placed a chair behind me, and gently attempted to make me sit down.

'Write to Diana and Mary tomorrow,' I said, 'and tell them to come home immediately. Diana said a small amount of money would make a difference to them, so with five thousand pounds each they will do very well.'

'Let me get you a glass of water,' said St John. 'You must really try and calm yourself.'

'Mr Rivers! You make me lose patience. I am reasonable enough.'

'Perhaps, if you explained yourself a little more fully–'

'Explain! What is there to explain? You must realize that twenty thousand pounds, divided equally among the four of us, will give five thousand pounds each. I am not blindly unjust or wickedly ungrateful. This money could never be all mine in justice, though it might be in law.'

'Jane, we will be your cousins without expecting this gift from you.'

'Cousins – I, wealthy, and you, poor!'

'And the school, Miss Eyre? It must now be shut up, I suppose?'

'No, I will keep my post of teacher until you find someone to take my place.'

He smiled approval, and left me.

I had many struggles and used many arguments before I got the money settled as I wished. It was hard work, but as I was determined to make a just division of the property, and since my cousins must in their own hearts have felt that I was only doing what they themselves would have done in my place, they gave way at last so far as to allow the affair to be judged by lawyers. My opinion received support, the necessary papers were written out and signed, and St John, Diana and Mary and I each became the possessors of a smallish fortune.

Chapter 38   Homecomings

It was near Christmas by the time all was settled and, when the holiday season arrived, I closed Morton School.

Mr Rivers came. I waited until all the classes, now numbering 60 girls, had left the building. Then I locked the door and stood with the key in my hand, exchanging words with some of my pupils.

'Do you consider that you have had your reward for a period

of hard work?' he asked, when they had gone. 'Would not a life given to the improvement of your race be well spent?'

'Yes,' I said, 'but I could not go on for ever in this way. I want to enjoy my own powers as well as to improve those of other people. I must enjoy them now; I am ready for a holiday. Don't remind me of school!'

He looked serious.

'What is this? What are you going to do?'

'To be active. I want you to let Hannah help me. Diana and Mary will be home in a week, and I want to have everything in order for their arrival.'

'I understand. I thought you were going off on some trip. Preparations in the house are all very well for the present, but I trust that later you will aim a little higher than the joys of housekeeping.'

Hannah and I worked hard. When the house had been well cleaned, I bought new furniture and rugs and spent a good deal of time arranging them.

The great day came at last. Hannah and I were dressed and everything was ready.

St John arrived first. He found me in the kitchen, watching the progress of some cakes baking for tea. Standing near the fire, he asked whether I was at last satisfied with servant's work. He then went away to the sitting room and began to read.

'They are coming! They are coming!' cried Hannah, throwing open the door. I ran out. The carriage had stopped at the gate. The driver opened the door. First one well-known figure, then another stepped out. They laughed and kissed me, then Hannah, and hurried into the house.

While the driver and Hannah brought in the luggage, they called for St John. At this moment he came out from the sitting room. They both threw their arms round his neck. He gave each one a quiet kiss, spoke a few words of welcome in a low voice, stood for a short while to be talked to, and then returned to the sitting room.

The evening was a happy one. My cousins were full of talk, and their conversation filled up their brother's silence. He was sincerely glad to see them, but he could not join in their good cheer.

The whole of the following week must have tested his patience. It was Christmas week, and we were happy and unsettled. The freedom of home, the country air, the coming of good fortune gave life to Diana and Mary, and they were cheerful from morning to night. St John kept away from us. He was rarely in the house, but found daily business in visiting the sick and poor in Morton.

As our happiness became calmer, we returned to our usual habits and regular studies. Mary drew, Diana read, and I worked at German. St John, who now stayed at home more, studied some strange language which was necessary for his future plans. He appeared quiet and busy enough, but his blue eye had a habit of leaving the strange-looking grammar and wandering over and fixing on me. I wondered what it meant. I wondered, too, at the continual satisfaction that he showed at my weekly visit to Morton School. If the weather was bad, and his sisters urged me not to go, he would always encourage me to do so. And when I returned, sometimes tired and wet from the rain, I never dared to complain, because I saw that this would annoy him.

One afternoon, though, I was allowed to stay at home, on account of a cold. His sisters had gone in my place. I sat translating; he sat working at his grammar. I found myself under the influence of his ever-watchful eye. It searched me through and through, sharply and coldly.

'Jane, what are you doing?'

'Learning German.'

'I want you to give up German and learn Hindustani.'

'You are not serious?'

'So serious that I will not allow you to refuse me. I will tell you why.'

He then went on to explain that Hindustani was the language that he himself was studying at present, in preparation for going to India to teach the word of God. As he moved onto higher lessons, he tended to forget the early ones. It would help him greatly to have a pupil with whom he might again go over the first lessons, and fix them thoroughly in his mind. Would I do this for him? I would not, perhaps, have to give up my time for long, as he expected to be leaving in three months' time.

St John was not a man to be easily refused. One felt that everything he experienced, whether pain or pleasure, had a deep and long-lasting effect on him. I agreed.

I found him a very patient yet severe master. He expected me to do a great deal. Gradually he gained a certain influence over me that took away my freedom of mind. I could no longer laugh or talk freely when he was near: I was conscious that only serious thoughts and behaviour were approved of. But I did not love my state of obedience, and I wished many times that he had continued to ignore me.

Chapter 39   'Jane! Jane! Jane!'

Not for a moment, in the middle of these changes of place and fortune, had I forgotten Mr Rochester. The desire to know what had happened to him followed me everywhere.

In the course of my letters to Mr Briggs about the money left me by my uncle, I had inquired whether he knew anything of Mr Rochester's present state, but he was quite without knowledge concerning him. I then wrote to Mrs Fairfax, begging for information on the subject. I was surprised when two weeks passed without reply, but when two months went by, and day after day the post brought nothing for me, I began to feel the sharpest anxiety.

I wrote again. There was a chance that my first letter had been lost. Hope returned for a few weeks, then disappeared. Not a line, not a word reached me. When I had waited unsuccessfully for half a year, my hope died completely, and then I felt truly sorrowful.

A fine spring shone around me, which I could not enjoy. Summer was coming. Diana tried to cheer me up. She said I looked ill, and wished to take me for a holiday by the sea. St John opposed this. He said I did not need amusement, but employment: my present life was too aimless. He continued with my lessons in Hindustani, and I, stupidly, could not refuse him.

One evening I had come to my studies feeling sadder than usual. Hannah had told me in the morning that the postman had left something for me, and when I went down to take it, almost certain that it was the desired news at last, I found only an unimportant letter from Mr Briggs on some matter of business. The bitter disappointment had drawn some tears from me, and now, as I sat struggling with the Indian writing, my eyes filled again.

St John called me to his side to read. In attempting to do this, my voice failed me. He and I were alone in the sitting room. My companion expressed no surprise at this show of feeling, nor did he question me as to its cause. He only said:

'We will wait for a few minutes, Jane, until you are calmer.'

Drying my eyes and murmuring something about not being very well, I returned to my lesson and succeeded in completing it. St John put away my books and his, locked his desk, and said:

'Jane, I want to have a talk with you.'

He remained silent for some minutes, and then went on:

'Jane, I leave in six weeks. I have booked my journey on a boat which sails on 20 June.'

I felt as if my future was shaping itself for me. I trembled to hear what he would say next. It came.

'Jane, come with me to India.'

The room seemed to spin round me.

'Oh, St John!' I cried. 'Have some pity!'

He continued:

'God and Nature intended you to be a clergyman's wife. You are formed for hard work, not for love. You must, you shall come with me. You shall be mine. I claim you for the service of God.'

'I am not fit,' I replied.

'I have an answer for you – hear it. I have watched you ever since we first met. I have seen you pass several tests of character. In the village school I found that you could perform, well and patiently, a job that was not to your taste or liking. By the calm with which you received the news that you had become rich, I saw that money had little influence over you. In the readiness with which you cut your fortune into four parts, and gave away three, I recognized that you could give up something of your own to others. In the obedience with which, at my wish, you gave up a study in which you were interested and began another because it interested me, I see a quality of the greatest use to my work. As a helper in Indian schools and among Indian women, you will be of great value to me.'

'I would not live long in such a country.'

'Ah! You are afraid for yourself,' he said scornfully.

'What do you mean?'

'I know where your heart is. The passion that you are keeping alive is against the law and religion. You are thinking of Mr Rochester.'

It was true. I admitted it by my silence.

The situation was very clear. In leaving England, I would leave a loved but empty land. Wherever Mr Rochester might be, he could be nothing to me. I must find another interest in life in place of the one I had lost, and what could be more useful and satisfying than that offered by St John?

'I could decide, if I were certain,' I said at last, 'if only I were sure that it is God's will.'

I sincerely desired to do what was right. 'Show me, show me the right path!' I prayed to heaven. I was more excited than I had ever been.

The whole house was still, as everyone except St John and myself had now gone upstairs to bed. The one candle was burnt out; the room was full of moonlight. My heart beat fast and heavily; I heard its movement. Suddenly it stood still as an inexpressible feeling ran through it. The feeling was not like an electric shock, but it was as sharp and as strange. It acted on my senses: my eye and ear waited, while the flesh trembled on my bones.

'What have you heard? What do you see?' asked St John.

I saw nothing, but I heard a voice somewhere cry:

'Jane! Jane! Jane!'

It did not seem to be in the room, nor in the house, nor in the garden. It did not come out of the air, nor from under the earth, nor from above me. I heard it, and it was the voice of a human being – a known, loved, well-remembered voice, that of Edward Rochester – and it spoke in pain, wildly and urgently.

'I am coming!' I cried. 'Wait for me! Oh, I will come!'

I flew to the door and looked into the passage. It was dark. I ran out into the garden. It was empty. 'Where are you?' I shouted.

The distant hills repeated my cry, but there was no reply.

St John had followed, but I asked him to leave me. He obeyed me immediately. It was my turn to command. I went up to my room, locked myself in, and fell on my knees in prayer. I rose with my mind made up, and lay down, waiting for the daylight.

Chapter 40   A Blackened Ruin

Daylight came. I rose and busied myself with arranging my things. I heard St John leave his room, open the door, and go outside.

It was still two hours to breakfast time. I spent the time walking up and down my room, and thinking over what had happened last night. I remembered that inner feeling that I had experienced, with all its indescribable strangeness. I remembered the voice that I had heard. Again I asked myself where it had come from, as uselessly as before. It had seemed to come from inside *me* – not from the outside world. I asked myself whether it was simply a nervous thought – a thing of the imagination. I could not believe this.

At breakfast I told Diana and Mary that I was going on a journey, and would be absent for at least four days.

'Alone, Jane?' they asked.

'Yes. It is to see or hear news of a friend about whom I have been anxious for some time.'

In their truly sensitive, delicate way, they asked no further questions, except that Diana asked me if I was sure I was well enough to travel.

I left the house at three o'clock and soon after four I stood at the foot of the signpost waiting for the coach that was to take me to distant Thornfield. In the silence of those lonely hills, I heard it coming from far away. It was the same coach which I had stepped down from a year ago, at this same place – how lonely and how hopeless! Now, as I entered and was once more on the road to Thornfield, I felt that I was going home.

It was a journey of 36 hours, and towards the end the scenery with its large fields and low hills, so much gentler than the area from which I had come, met my eye like the features of a familiar face. The coach stopped at a small hotel, and I spoke to a servant who came out.

'How far is it to Thornfield Hall from here?' I asked.

'Just two miles across the fields.'

I got out of the coach, and left my box at the hotel. The early morning light shone on the signboard, and I read in gold letters, "The Rochester Arms". My heart beat with joy; I was already on my master's lands. It became quiet again as the thought came to me:

'Your master may not be here, and even if he is, you can have nothing to do with him. You had better go no further. Ask for information from the people at the hotel.'

The suggestion was reasonable, but I could not make myself accept it. I feared a reply that would crush me with despair. I wanted to look once more at the Hall. There was the stile in front of me, the fields, and the path. Almost before I had realized what I was doing, I was on the way. How fast I walked! How I looked ahead to catch the first sight of the well-known woods!

At last they appeared before me. I hurried on. Another field, a track, and there were the walls of the kitchen garden and the buildings at the back. The house itself was still hidden.

'My first view will be of the front,' I decided, 'where I can see my master's window. Perhaps he will be standing at it – he rises early. Perhaps he is even now walking in the garden. If I could just see him. Surely, in that case, I would not be so mad as to run to him?'

I had passed along the walls of the kitchen garden, and turned the corner. There was a gate beyond, between two stone pillars. I put my head slowly round one of them.

I looked with fearful joy towards a great house. I saw a blackened ruin, with the silence of death about it.

Chapter 41 Death and Destruction

I had to have some answers to the questions that rushed through my mind. I could find them nowhere except at the hotel, and so I returned there.

The manager himself brought the meal that I had ordered.

'You know Thornfield Hall, of course?' I managed to ask him at last.

'Yes, I was in Mr Rochester's service until his death.'

'Death!' I cried. 'Is he really dead?'

'I mean the father of the present gentleman, Mr Edward.'

I breathed again.

'Is Mr Rochester living at the Hall now?'

'Oh, no! Thornfield Hall was burnt down last autumn. A terrible event! So much valuable property was destroyed. The fire broke out in the middle of the night. It was a fearful sight.'

In the middle of the night! That was always the hour of mysterious happenings at Thornfield.

'Do they know how it started?'

'They guessed, they guessed. You may not perhaps know,' he continued, moving a little closer, and speaking in a low voice, 'that there was a lady, a – a madwoman, kept in the house?'

'I have heard something of it.'

'This lady,' he went on, 'was found to be Mr Rochester's wife. It was discovered in the strangest way. There was a young lady, a governess at the Hall, that Mr Rochester was in–'

'But the fire–' I suggested.

'I'm coming to that – a governess that Mr Rochester was in love with. The servants say they never saw anyone so much in love as he was. She was a small thing, they say, almost like a child. Well, he was determined to marry her.'

'You shall tell me this part of the story another time,' I said, 'but now I have a particular reason for wishing to hear all about

142

the fire. Was it suspected that this madwoman was the cause of it?'

'It's quite certain that she started it. She had a woman to take care of her, called Mrs Poole, very dependable, except for one fault – she sometimes took strong drink and fell asleep, and then the madwoman would steal her keys and escape. On this night the madwoman set fire first to the curtains in the room next to her own, and then got down to a lower floor and burnt the bed in the room that had belonged to the governess, but it was empty, fortunately. The governess had run away two months before, and although Mr Rochester searched for her as if she were the most valuable thing in the world, he never heard a word of her, and he became quite wild with his disappointment. He wanted to be alone. He sent Mrs Fairfax, his housekeeper, to friends of hers a long way away. Miss Adèle, a little girl who was in his charge, was sent to school. He refused to visit any of his neighbours, and shut himself up in the house.'

'What! Didn't he leave England?'

'Leave England! He did not move out of doors, except at night, when he walked like a ghost about the garden, as if he were out of his mind – which it is my opinion he was, because I never saw a prouder, more strong-willed gentleman than he was before that governess upset him. He was not very good-looking, but he had a courage and a strength of mind of his own.'

'Then Mr Rochester was at home when the fire broke out?'

'Yes, certainly he was. He went up to the back rooms on the top floor when everything was burning above and below, and got the servants out safely, and then went back to get his mad wife out of her room. And then they called out to him that she was on the roof, where she was standing, waving her arms and shouting. She was a big woman, with long black hair. We could see it blowing against the flames as she stood. We saw him climb up to the roof. We heard him call, "Bertha!" We saw him move closer to her, and then she screamed and jumped and the next minute she lay still on the ground below.'

'Dead?'

'Dead! Yes, as dead as the stones on which her brains and blood lay scattered. It was terrible!'

'Were any other lives lost?'

'No – perhaps it would have been better if there had been.'

'What do you mean?'

'Poor Mr Edward! Some say he deserved it for keeping his first marriage secret and wanting to take another wife while he had one living – but I pity him, myself.'

'You said he was alive?'

'Yes, he is alive, but many think he would be better dead.'

'Why? How?' My blood was again running cold.

'He is blind.'

I had feared worse. I had feared that he was mad. I called up my strength to ask the cause of his suffering.

'It was all his own courage and kindness. He wouldn't leave the house until everyone else was out before him. As he came down the great staircase, the roof fell in. He was taken out from under the ruins, alive, but badly hurt. One eye was knocked out, and one hand so crushed that the doctor had to take it off immediately. He lost the sight of the other eye as well.'

'Where is he? Where does he live now?'

'At Ferndean, a country house on a farm that he owns, about 30 miles away.'

'Who is with him?'

'Two old servants. He refused to have more. He is quite destroyed, they say.'

'Have you any sort of carriage?'

'We have a very fine one.'

'Let it be got ready immediately, and if your driver can get me to Ferndean before dark today, I'll pay both you and him twice the money you usually demand.'

Chapter 42   Magic

The house of Ferndean was a fairly large building hidden deep in a wood. I had heard of it before. Mr Rochester had often spoken of it, and had sometimes visited it. His father had bought the property because he enjoyed shooting there. He would have let the house, but could find no one to rent it because of its inconvenient and unhealthy position. It therefore remained unlived-in and without furniture, except for two or three rooms fitted up for the use of the owner when he went there to shoot.

It was just before dark on an evening characterized by a dull sky, cold wind, and continual light rain. I dismissed the carriage and walked the last mile. Even when I was within a very short distance of the house, I could see nothing of it because the trees grew so thick and dark around it.

At last my path became clear, and I stood in an area of enclosed ground in front of the house, which could hardly be seen in the faint light. There were no flowers, no garden, and everything was still except for the gentle fall of the rain.

'Can there be life here?' I asked myself.

Yes, there was life of some kind. I heard a movement. The narrow front door was opening.

It opened slowly. A figure came out into the half-light and stood on the step, a man without a hat, who stretched out his hand as if to feel whether it rained. Though it was growing dark, I recognized him – it was my master, Edward Rochester, and no other.

I paused, almost held my breath, and stood to watch him – to examine him, myself unseen, and ah! unable to be seen by him. It was a sudden meeting, and one in which joy was balanced by pain.

His form was the same strong one as ever, his walk still upright, his hair still black. His features were unchanged. But in his face I saw a change: he looked despairing, like some wronged and caged wild animal or bird, dangerous to come close to in his sorrow.

He climbed down the one step, and moved slowly towards the grass. Then he paused, as if he did not know which way to turn. He lifted his hand and opened his eyelids, and looked with difficulty up at the sky and towards the trees. I saw that to him it was all empty darkness.

At this moment John, the servant, joined him.

'Will you take my arm, sir? There is heavy rain coming on. Hadn't you better go in?'

'Leave me alone,' was the answer.

John went in without having noticed me. Mr Rochester, after trying unsuccessfully to walk around, felt his way back into the house.

I now followed and knocked. John's wife opened the door, then stepped back as if she had seen a ghost.

I calmed her, and followed her into the kitchen, explaining in a few words that I had just heard what had happened since I left Thornfield. At this moment the bell in the sitting room rang.

The servant filled a glass with water, and placed it on a table with some candles.

'Is that what he rang for?' I asked.

'Yes, he always has candles brought in when it gets dark, though he is blind.'

'Let me take them. I will carry them in.'

I took them from the table. My hand shook as I held them. The water ran from the glass, and my heart beat loudly and fast. John's wife opened the sitting room door, and shut it behind me.

The room did not look cheerful. A small fire burnt low in the fireplace, and leaning over it was the blind owner of the house. His old dog, Pilot, lay on one side, but jumped up and ran joyfully to me as I came in, almost knocking the water from my hand. I set it on the table, and said softly, 'Lie down!' Mr Rochester turned to see what had excited Pilot, but, remembering his weakness, turned his head back again.

'Give me the water,' he said.

I moved closer to him. Pilot followed me, still excited.

'Down, Pilot!' I said again. He paused with the water halfway to his lips.

'Who is this? Who is this?' he demanded. 'Answer me – speak again!'

'Pilot knows me, and John and his wife. I have just arrived,' I answered.

He put out his hand with a quick movement. Not seeing where I stood, he did not touch me. I put my hand in his.

'Her fingers!' he cried. 'Is it Jane?' He seized my arm, my shoulder, my waist. 'This is her shape – this is her size–'

'And this is her voice,' I added. 'She is all here: her heart, too. God save you, sir! I am glad to be so near you again.'

'You are real? You are a human being? My living Jane? You are certain of that?'

'I truly believe so, Mr Rochester.'

'But how, on this dark evening, could you appear so suddenly in my lonely room? I stretched out my hand to take a glass of water from a servant, and it was given me by you. I asked a question, and your voice spoke in my ear.'

'Because I came in with the water and candles in place of John's wife.'

'There is magic in this hour. Who can tell what a dark, hopeless life I have led for the past months? Doing nothing, expecting nothing, conscious only of an unending sorrow, and at times a mad desire to see my Jane again. How can it be that Jane is with me? Will she not go away as suddenly as she came?'

I was sure that talk of ordinary matters was best for him in this state of mind. I asked him when he had his supper.

'I never have supper.'

'But you shall have some tonight. I am hungry, and so are you, I expect – only you forget.'

Calling John's wife, I soon had a meal on the table, and a more cheerful fire. I was excited, and I talked to him with relaxed pleasure during supper and for a long time after that. There was no feeling of awkwardness, no holding back of life and laughter. With him I was happy, because I knew I suited him. Though he was blind, smiles began to light up his face, and his features lost their look of bitterness.

'Whom have you been with all this time, Jane?'

'You shall not find that out from me tonight, sir. You must wait until tomorrow. Now I'll leave you. I have been travelling for three days, and I believe I am tired. Good night.'

'Just one word, Jane. Were there only ladies in the house where you have been?'

I laughed and went away. I could see now the means of driving away his sadness.

Chapter 43   Past and Future

Very early the next morning I heard him go downstairs. As soon as the servants came down, I heard the question, 'Is Miss Eyre here?' Then, 'Which room did you put her in? Is she up? Go and ask her if she wants anything, and when she will come down.'

Entering the breakfast room very softly, I had a view of him before he discovered my presence. He sat in his chair, the lines of now customary sadness marking his strong features.

'It is a bright sunny morning, sir,' I said. 'The rain is over. You must go for a walk.'

I had driven away his sadness. He smiled.

Most of the morning was spent out of doors. After a time he

148

urged me to tell him about my experiences during the last year. I began my story, but I softened the description of my three days of wandering a good deal.

He told me that I should not have left him in that way, without any means of supporting myself. He was certain that I had suffered more than I had admitted to him.

'Well, whatever my sufferings were, they were short,' I answered. I then told of my welcome by the Rivers family, and of all that followed.

'This St John, then, is your cousin?'

'Yes.'

'You have spoken of him often. Do you like him?'

'He is a very good man, sir. I could not help liking him.'

'A good man. Does that mean a respectable man of fifty?'

'St John is only twenty-nine, sir.'

'Is he a dull person, short and ugly?'

'He is a good-looking man: tall, fair, with blue eyes.'

'But his brain? It is probably rather soft?'

'He talks little, sir, but what he says is always worth listening to. He is a truly intelligent man.'

'Did you like him, Jane?'

'Yes, Mr Rochester, I liked him. But you asked me that before.'

Jealousy had got hold of him, but the sting was bringing him back to life.

'Did he visit you often at your school?'

'Daily.'

'You had a small house near the school, you say. Did he ever come there to see you?'

'Sometimes.'

A pause.

'Did Rivers spend much time with the ladies of the family while you were living with them?'

'Yes, we worked in the same room.'

149

'What did you study?'

'I learnt German, at first.'

'Did he teach you?'

'He does not understand German. He taught me a little Hindustani.'

'Rivers taught you Hindustani?'

'Yes, sir.'

'And his sisters too?'

'No, only me.'

'Did you ask to learn?'

'No, he wished to teach me.'

'Why did he wish it? Of what use could Hindustani be to you?'

'He intended me to go to India with him.'

'He wanted to marry you?'

'He asked me to marry him.'

'That is an invention, to annoy me.'

'I beg your pardon, sir. He did ask me, and was as serious in urging me as ever you could be.'

'Miss Eyre, you can leave me. Go and marry this Rivers.'

'He will never be my husband. He does not love me, and I do not love him. He wanted me only because he thought I would make a suitable clergyman's wife. He is good and great, but too cold for me. Must I leave you, sir, to go to him?'

'What, Jane! Is that really how things are?'

'Really, sir.'

'You wish to be friends, Jane?'

'Yes, sir.'

'Ah, Jane, but I want a wife.'

'Do you, sir?'

'Yes. Is it news to you?'

'Choose then, sir – her who loves you best.'

'I will at least choose – her whom I love best. Jane, will you marry me?'

'Yes, sir.'

'A poor blind man, whom you will have to lead about by the hand?'

'Most truly, sir.'

A little later, he said:

'Jane, a strange thing happened to me a few days ago. It was last Monday night. I had long had the belief that, since I could not find you, you must be dead. Late that night I began to pray for death too. My punishment, I felt, had lasted long enough: I asked God to end it so that I could be admitted to that world to come, where there was still hope of joining you. My heart's wishes broke from my lips in the words – "Jane! Jane! Jane!"

'You will think that I imagined things, but what I tell you now is true. As I called, a voice, I cannot tell from where, replied: "I am coming! Wait for me!" and a moment later the words, "Where are you?" were whispered on the wind. In spirit, I believe, we must have met.'

Chapter 44   The End

I married Mr Rochester very quietly a few days later, and wrote immediately to my cousins to say what I had done. Diana and Mary approved my action immediately. How St John received the news, I do not know. He never answered the letter that I sent him on the subject. Six months later he wrote to me calmly and kindly, but without mentioning Mr Rochester's name. He has since written regularly, though not frequently, from India, where he is giving his life to his work.

I soon went to visit little Adèle at her school. Her wild joy at seeing me again filled me with pity. She looked pale and thin. I found the rules of the school too severe for a child of her age, and I took her home with me until I could find a more suitable place of education. When she left school, I found her a pleasing and grateful companion.

Mr Rochester remained blind for the first two years of our marriage. Then, one morning, as I was writing a letter for him, he said:

'Jane, have you something shiny around your neck?'

I was wearing a gold chain. I answered, 'Yes.'

'And have you a pale blue dress on?'

I had. He then informed me that he had thought for some time that the darkness clouding one eye was becoming lighter, and that now he was sure of it.

He and I went up to London. He took the advice of a famous eye doctor, and in time regained the sight of one eye. He cannot see very clearly, but when his son was first put into his arms, he could see that the boy had his own eyes as they once were – large, bright and black.

Diana and Mary Rivers are both married, and come to see us every year. Diana's husband is a captain in the navy; Mary's a clergyman, a college friend of her brother's.

St John is unmarried. He will never marry now. The last letter I received from him showed only too clearly that his work on this earth is nearly over. He has no fear of death, and when his end comes, it will be as he has wished.

ACTIVITIES

Chapters 1–5

Before you read

1 Look at the Word List at the back of this book.
   a Which of these words are used when talking about children?
   governess   guardian   nursery   obedience   stile   veil
   b Which of these words are for people?
   bride   clergyman   committee   companion   gipsy   people
   c Which of these words are for feelings?
   carriage   grief   misery   passion   scorn   suspicion

2 Read the Introduction to this book, and answer the questions.
   a What is Jane's job at Thornfield Hall?
   b Who is her employer?
   c What has happened to her parents?
   d Where was she brought up?

While you read

3 Answer the questions. Who:
   a hits Jane regularly?   ....
   b is punished for fighting?   ....
   c is Jane afraid of in the red room?   ....
   d thinks that Jane might die?   ....
   e suggests a solution to Jane's problems?   ....
   f accuses Mrs Reed of cruelty?   ....

After you read

4 Match the names with the descriptions.
   a Jane Eyre   ..... **1)** Jane's cruel aunt
   b Bessie   ..... **2)** a children's nurse
   c John Reed   ..... **3)** a kind man who sells medicine
   d Mrs Reed   ..... **4)** a ten-year-old orphan
   e Abbot   ..... **5)** Jane's dead father, a poor clergyman
   f Mr Lloyd   ..... **6)** Jane's cruel fourteen-year-old cousin
   g Mr Eyre   ..... **7)** a servant girl at Gateshead
   h Mr Brocklehurst   ..... **8)** the director of Lowood Institution

5 Why are these important to Jane's story?

   a the red room

   b ghosts

   c Mr Lloyd

   d Jane's feelings for Aunt Reed and her cousins

   e Jane's departure for school

6 Discuss how the relationship between Jane and Aunt Reed changes after the decision is made that Jane will go away to school.

Chapters 6–10

Before you read

7 Discuss these questions.

   a Do you think Jane will find happiness at Lowood? Why (not)?

   b In what ways will Lowood be better or worse for Jane than Gateshead, do you think?

While you read

8 Are these sentences true (T) or false (F)?

   a The teachers are happy with the way Mr
   Brocklehurst runs Lowood Institution.   .....

   b Care and education at the school are free.   .....

   c Children are punished for small offences.   .....

   d Miss Temple is a kind, interesting teacher.   .....

   e Helen's courage helps Jane.   .....

   f Miss Temple believes that Jane is a liar.   .....

   g Jane preferred Gateshead to Lowood.   .....

   h Helen dies of a fever.   .....

After you read

9 Who is said by whom to:

   a live in 'a world of private dreams'?

   b be 'full of goodness'?

   c be 'a servant of the Devil' and 'a liar'?

   d be 'very happy' and 'at rest'?

10 Discuss with another student the differences between:

    a Jane's life at Gateshead and her life at Lowood.

    b Miss Temple and Mr Brocklehurst.

    c Helen Burns and Jane Eyre.

11 Work with another student and have this conversation.

    Student A: You are Helen Burns and you are dying. Tell Jane how you feel and give Jane advice about how to be happy.

    Student B: You are Jane Eyre and you are at Helen's bedside. Tell Helen why you will miss her and how she has helped you.

Chapters 11–17

Before you read

12 Discuss these questions.

    a How useful do you think Mr Lloyd's idea was, that Jane should leave her aunt's house? What, if anything, will she gain from her stay at the orphanage?

    b Why do you think the fever at Lowood Institution spread so fast and caused so many deaths? What do you think will happen at the school as a result?

    c What do you think will happen to Jane when she is too old to stay at the orphanage?

While you read

13 Write the names of the characters.

    a .... remains at Lowood for eight years.

    b .... replies to Jane's advertisement.

    c .... is Jane's young pupil.

    d .... is Jane's new employer, the owner of Thornfield and Adèle's guardian.

    e .... is a servant who is said to be responsible for a ghostlike laugh.

14 Who is talking? What are they talking about?

    a 'Ah, the governess!'

    b 'He came with master.'

    c 'Does my forehead not please you?'

    d 'It is never too late to mend things.'

    e 'Did you plan to drown me?'

    f 'It would be wise to do so.'

    g '. . . strong features, large black eyes as black as her jewels . . .'

    h 'Picture of a governess, poor and plain.'

After you read

15 Discuss what Jane thinks about:

    a the sound of the laughter from upstairs.

    b Mr Rochester's behaviour towards her.

    c Mr Rochester sharing his secret about Adèle with her.

    d Mr Rochester's failure to punish Grace for trying to kill him.

    e her feelings for Mr Rochester after he leaves for the Leas.

16 Work with another student and have this conversation.

    Student A: You are Jane Eyre and it is the morning after the fire. You see Grace Poole in Mr Rochester's bedroom sewing curtains. You decide to test her. Ask questions about the events of the previous night.

    Student B: You are Grace Poole. Find out what Jane knows. Answer her questions, but without telling her anything.

Chapters 18–22

Before you read

17 Discuss these questions.

    a How does Jane think that comparing a drawing of herself with one of Blanche will help her? Will it? Why (not)?

    b Read the titles of Chapters 18–22. What do you think will happen next?

18 Put these events in the correct order, 1–6.

    a The gipsy fortune-teller asks to see Jane Eyre. .....

    b Mr Mason arrives at Thornfield Hall from the West
Indies. .....

    c Mr Rochester returns to Thornfield Hall with Lady
Ingram and her daughters. .....

    d Jane discovers that the gipsy is really Mr Rochester. .....

    e Jane admits to herself that she is in love with Mr
Rochester. .....

    f Mr Rochester tells Jane that he would like to be alone
with her. .....

19 What does Mr Rochester do? Tick (✓) the correct sentences.

    a He lies to his guests to make them return to their beds. .....

    b He leaves Jane on the top floor with Mason and Grace
Poole. .....

    c He forbids any conversation between Grace Poole and
Jane. .....

    d He returns quickly with a doctor. .....

After you read

20 Discuss these questions.

    a Why does Mr Rochester pretend to be a fortune-teller?

    b What does Jane think has happened to Mason on the top
floor?

Chapters 23–28

Before you read

21 What do you think is the relationship between Grace Poole and Mr
Rochester, and between Mr Rochester and Mason? Why are they
all behaving so mysteriously?

22 Write the missing word in each sentence.

    a Mason's wounds come from a woman's ....

    b Mr Rochester says that Thornfield is like a ....

    c He is worried that careless talk by .... will destroy his chance of happiness.

    d Jane learns that her cousin John has ....

    e Jane's aunt is ill and wants to .... her.

    f Jane wants to leave Thornfield before Mr Rochester's .... enters the house.

    g Jane learns from a letter that her .... wanted her to live with him in Madeira.

    h Mr Rochester deceives Jane to make her .... her true feelings for him.

    i In the middle of the night, somebody tears Jane's .... in two.

After you read

23 Discuss what happens the night that Mr Rochester is away on business just before the wedding day. What does Jane dream? What happens in her bedroom? Who do you think tears the veil and why?

Chapters 29–34

Before you read

24 Discuss why Mr Rochester wants to wait a year before he tells Jane about Grace Poole. Why does Jane agree to this?

While you read

25 Answer these questions. Write YES or NO.

    a Do Mr Rochester and Jane get married in the church near Thornfield? .....

    b Can Mr Rochester legally marry anyone? .....

    c Did he choose Bertha Mason himself? .....

    d Is Bertha mad? .....

    e Did Jane's uncle know about her wedding plans? .....

26 Put these events in the correct order, 1–5.

    a Jane finds herself in the house of the Rivers family.   .....

    b Jane leaves Thornfield.   .....

    c Jane accepts a job teaching poor girls.   .....

    d The Rivers family learn that their Uncle John has died.   .....

    e Jane leaves her few possessions in the coach.   .....

After you read

27 Discuss the unfortunate circumstances of Mr Rochester's marriage to Bertha Mason and how his marriage to Jane Eyre became known to Richard Mason. Who is most to blame for the unhappiness in Mr Rochester's life?

28 Why do Mary and Diana not feel sad about their Uncle John's death? Is this a familiar situation in the story?

Chapters 35–44

Before you read

29 Discuss these questions.

    a Do you think that Jane's past will help her in her new job? If so, how?

    b Do you think Jane will ever see Mr Rochester again? Will she fall in love with her new employer?

While you read

30 Circle the correct word in these sentences.

    a St John tears a piece of paper from Jane's painting because he sees *Jane Elliot / Jane Eyre* written on it.

    b Mr Briggs, a lawyer, has been searching for Jane Eyre because her uncle in Madeira has left her his *debts / property*.

    c Jane shares her fortune with her new *cousins / friends*.

    d Jane agrees to learn *Hindustani / German* from St John, who needs to learn it himself.

    e St John asks Jane to go to *Thornfield / India*.

    f Jane finds that Thornfield has been destroyed and that Mr Rochester is now *mad / blind*.

After you read

31 Answer the questions.

    a What does Jane do with the money that she receives from her uncle? Why?

    b What does St John Rivers mean when he tells Jane that the passion she is keeping alive (for Mr Rochester) is against the law and religion?

32 Work with another student and act out this conversation, ten years after the events in this story.

    Student A: You are the son of Mr Rochester and Jane. Ask your mother how she and your father met, and how they married.

    Student B: You are Jane. Answer your son's questions, but protect him from information that would upset him.

33 Discuss how passion, grief, misery and prayer bring Jane and Mr Rochester together.

Writing

34 Write a comparison of Charlotte Brontë's life with Jane Eyre's.

35 Write a report about how the changes made to Lowood Institution under its new management improved the children's lives.

36 Write the letter from the committee at Lowood Institution to Mrs Fairfax at Thornfield Hall, describing Jane's character and teaching experience. Give a good recommendation so that Mrs Fairfax will want to employ Jane.

37 Write a letter from Mr Rochester to Blanche Ingram explaining why he will not marry her but will marry Jane instead.

38 Choose a character from the story and write what you would have done differently if you had been that person. Explain why.

39 Write a report for the local newspaper of the fire that destroyed Thornfield Hall, explaining how it started and what resulted.

40 List the three most important people in Jane Eyre's life, and the reasons for their importance.

41 Compare Jane's Reed relations with her Rivers relations. Give reasons for their different behaviour towards Jane.

42 Write a report on this book. Tell the story in one or two paragraphs. Explain why you did or did not enjoy it.

43 Write a report for a magazine explaining how poverty changes a person and a family. What is society's responsibility to the poor, in your opinion?

WORD LIST

approve (v) to believe that someone or something is acceptable; to agree to something

awkward (adj) embarrassed and shy; difficult to deal with

bride (n) a woman who is getting married, or who has just been married

candle (n) a stick of wax that gives light when it burns

carriage (n) a vehicle pulled by horses

clergyman (n) a male priest

coach (n) a closed vehicle with four wheels pulled by horses, which people travelled in

committee (n) a group of people who meet regularly to do a job or make decisions

companion (n) someone who you spend a lot of time with

gipsy (n) a member of a race of people who travel from place to place

governess (n) a woman who lives with a family and teaches their children at home

groan (n/v) a long, deep sound, usually made by someone in pain

grief (n) a feeling of extreme sadness, especially after someone has died

guardian (n) someone who is legally responsible for another person's child

heir (n) someone who has the legal right to receive the property of a person who has died

lungs (n pl) the two parts of your body that you use for breathing

misery (n) a feeling of great unhappiness

murmur (n/v) a soft quiet sound made by someone's voice

nursery (n) a young child's room; a **nursery story** is a story for young children

obedience (n) the act of obeying a person, law or rule

passion (n) a very strong feeling, usually of love or of belief in something

pillar (n) a tall, solid support for a building

rug (n) a piece of thick cloth or wool that is put on the floor as decoration

Better learning
comes from fun.

Pearson English **Readers**

There are plenty of Pearson English Readers to choose from
- world classics, film and television adaptations, short stories, thrillers,
modern-day crime and adventure, biographies, American classics,
non-fiction, plays ... and more to come.

For a complete list of all Pearson English Readers titles, please contact
your local Pearson Education office or visit the website.

pearsonenglishreaders.com

scorn (n) an opinion that someone or something is stupid or worthless

severe (adj) angry or strict

stile (n) part of a fence that is specially designed so that you can climb over it

suspicion (n) the feeling that someone has done something wrong or that something may be true

tremble (v) to shake because you are worried, afraid or excited

veil (n) a thin piece of material that women wear to cover their faces; something that it is difficult to see through

wicked (adj) behaving in a way that is morally very bad